first time
WINDOW TREATMENTS

Brimming with creative inspiration, how-to projects, and useful information to enrich your everyday life, Quarto Knows is a favorite destination for those pursuing their interests and passions. Visit our site and dig deeper with our books into your area of interest: Quarto Creates, Quarto Cooks, Quarto Homes, Quarto Lives, Quarto Drives, Quarto Explores, Quarto Gifts, or Quarto Kids.

First Published in 2019 by Quarry Books, an imprint of The Quarto Group,
100 Cummings Center, Suite 265-D, Beverly, MA 01915, USA.
T (978) 282-9590 F (978) 283-2742 QuartoKnows.com

Quarry Books titles are also available at discount for retail, wholesale, promotional, and bulk purchase. For details, contact the Special Sales Manager by email at specialsales@quarto.com or by mail at The Quarto Group, Attn: Special Sales Manager, 100 Cummings Center, Suite 265-D, Beverly, MA 01915, USA.

10 9 8 7 6 5 4 3 2 1

ISBN: 978-1-63159-785-5

Digital edition published in 2019

The content in this book previously appeared in the book SINGER® *Sewing Custom Curtains, Shades, and Top Treatments* (Creative Publishing International 2016) by Susan Woodcock.

Library of Congress Cataloging-in-Publication Data available

Design and Page Layout: Megan Jones Design
Cover Image: Susan Woodcock
Photography: Susan Woodcock, except for the following pages; 7, 32, Sandy Kozar; 37, Diana Apgar; 39, Terry Varner; 60, Barbara Elliott and Jennifer Ward Woods, 108, Tonie VanderHulst; 110, Suzan Wemlinger (all of Decorating Den Interiors)
Illustration: Susan Woodcock

Printed in China

first time
WINDOW TREATMENTS

THE ABSOLUTE BEGINNER'S GUIDE

by Susan Woodcock

QUARRY

contents

introduction

Interior decoration is an important part of every home. Soft furnishings like curtains, bedding, and upholstery can create beautiful rooms filled with pattern, color, and texture. But there is also a practical side. Fabric furnishings can improve your quality of living, making your home inviting, safe, and comfortable.

Creating your own window coverings can be very rewarding. You will feel accomplished and proud of your skills, and save money. That is not to say that making your own window treatments is cheap. The fabric, supplies, and hard-ware that you will need to complete your project can be a big investment. But if you are willing to devote the time and effort to planning and making them properly, your window treatments will last for many, many years. Money well spent!

This book is designed to give you added confidence as you learn basic to intermediate skills. With each new project you will gain experience, and soon you will be able to tackle any type of window treatment.

GETTING STARTED

Making window treatments is different than other types of sewing. You are hanging fabric at a window. Windows are large! It can be intimidating, but most of the sewing techniques are basic and easy to learn. You can start out with basic tools and supplies, and in this section you will learn tips for setting up your workspace to make sewing large projects easier. Let's get started!

setting up a workspace

Before you begin cutting and sewing, you will need to set up a functional workspace. If you do not have a sewing room, create a designated space for working on your project. Because of the size of window treatments, and the amount of fabric you will be handling, it's most helpful to have a large, sturdy worktable. In fact, it is perhaps the most important tool for making window treatments!

In a professional workroom you will find large worktables 60 inches (152 cm) wide by 10 to 12 feet (3 to 3.7 m) long. The tops are covered with canvas stretched over an underlayment for pinning and a thin layer of dense batting. This provides a large cutting and ironing surface, and fabrics can be secured by sticking pins into the underlayment.

You can make a temporary worktable with a dining or Ping-Pong table covered in foam interlocking floor tiles and a quilt, secured with tape or ties under the sides and corners. For a more permanent sewing table, cover plywood with ceiling tiles or insulation board for pinning, top with thin batting, and then stretch heavy canvas over the top, stapling it under the edges. You can place this on top of folding tables with nonskid rug pads to prevent slipping, or secure it to shelving units or even sawhorses. This is much better than trying to work on the floor.

A professional workroom is set up with worktables, fabric racks, a variety of machines, and organized tools and supplies. Photo is courtesy of Frances Pusch Fine Sewing for Interiors (www.FrancesPusch.com).

Make sure you have adequate lighting and ventilation. If you are working in a garage or basement with concrete floors, use foam tiles or anti-fatigue mats where you will be standing.

Set up sewing machines so there is plenty of room to manipulate large pieces of fabric. Additional folding tables can help hold the weight and keep fabrics off the floor. A functional and comfortable workspace will make sewing window treatments easier and more enjoyable.

tools and supplies

You can begin sewing window treatments with common, everyday sewing notions and tools. The good news is that you can get started today! As you gain experience and tackle more complex styles you will need to invest in specialty tools and supplies.

An industrial sewing machine is not required, although it certainly is helpful for sewing heavy fabrics. If your machine has a compensating foot or walking foot, you will find that to be very useful.

Review the list to become familiar with common workroom materials, tools, and supplies.

MATERIALS

Blackout: A lining material that has been treated to block all light. Look for a three-pass blackout material for complete light blocking.

Buckram: Traditionally a woven cotton cloth stiffened with starch (aka crinoline) but modern versions can be made from polyester or heavy paper. Used to add structure in curtain and valance headings for crisp pleats. Buckram is available in different widths and sew-on or iron-on. The most common width is 4 inches (10.2 cm).

Bump cloth: A very heavy, blanket-like interlining commonly used in silk for a luxurious finish.

Dim out: A light-blocking material for lining window treatments. It is often called thermal lining. This material has a suede-like surface that helps diffuse light.

Hook-and-loop tape: Pressure-sensitive tape like Velcro is used to attach window treatments to boards and in other areas where the fabrics need to be removable yet securely fastened.

Blackout lining

Interlining

Interfacing: A woven or nonwoven material for adding body or stabilizing fabrics.

Interlining: Usually flannel but can be any fabric that is sandwiched between the face fabric and the lining.

Lining: A cotton, polyester, or cotton and polyester blend fabric used to cover the reverse side of a window treatment. Look for a lining material that is specifically finished for window treatments; they will perform better than other fabrics. The most common colors of lining fabrics are white, ivory, and khaki.

Pleating and shirring tapes: Sew-on tapes with cords used to make curtains and valances. When the cords are pulled, the fabric makes even pleats, tucks, or gathers. These tapes can have one, two, three, or more cords depending on the style.

Welt cord: Also known as piping; a cord that is covered in fabric and used to finish seams. Welt cord can be made of soft fibers, like cotton or polyester, or firm, with cellulose for upholstery or polypropylene for outdoor use. It comes in a wide range of diameters. Micro welt cord is made with cable cord.

A variety of welt cords.

SUPPLIES

Bead weight: Also called sausage weight; tiny weights that are encased inside a woven strip and added to the bottom curtains for an even weight across the entire hem. Bead weight can also be covered and used in place of welt cord in seams.

Fabric glue: A wet adhesive used to secure fabrics together and to apply trims. Fabric glue will seep into the fibers and when dry creates an excellent bond.

Hand-sewing supplies: Needles such as long darners are suitable for sewing hems and applying trims. Curved needles are useful for awkward areas where a regular needle will not work. Thread should be strong and stable without any stretching. Hand-quilting thread is ideal for sewing hems and trims and tacking Roman shade rings. Thimbles will make hand sewing easier. Use the type of thimble that you are most comfortable with: metal, plastic, or leather.

Iron-on fusing web: A quick and easy product for joining two fabrics together temporarily before sewing, or permanently for no-sew hems.

Low-tack tape: Blue painter's tape can be used to mark placement of inset trims, or as a sewing guide applied next to the presser foot on your machine.

Machine-sewing supplies: Keep a variety of needles for different weights of fabric. Use general-purpose thread for most fabrics and heavy-weight thread for multiple thicknesses and upholstery-weight fabrics.

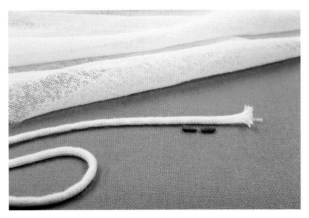

Bead weight has small pieces of weight encased in a sleeve.

Markers: Keep a good assortment of markers for different colors and weights of fabrics, and for making patterns. Chalk markers come in both solid pieces and pencil styles. Disappearing or erasable markers are good for marking Roman shade rings, seam lines on face fabrics, or other areas where a temporary mark is needed. Use pencils for marking cut lengths and permanent markers when drafting paper patterns.

Pin hooks: Sharp, angled hooks that are designed specifically for hanging curtains and valances. The sharp hooks are more common and easy to adjust, but you can also find traditional sew-on hooks.

Pins: Long pins are needed for the thickness of layers. Glass-head straight pins will tolerate ironing. T-pins and heavy-duty pushpins are used for holding fabrics in place for stapling.

Shade sewing supplies: Shades require an assortment of supplies such as rings, ribs, and other items. See the section on shades for more specific information.

Tack strip: Cardboard strip used in upholstery, stapled under fabrics to create a crisp edge.

Weight tape: Square weights sewn into a wide tape. Most commonly used in hems of stage curtains and other heavy, large projects.

Drapery weights: Metal pieces that are square, round, or triangular in shape and added to hems and seams to help window treatments hang properly. Traditionally, weights are made of lead, but newer versions are made of non-lead metal compounds and are safer for the environment.

Pin hooks

TOOLS

Clamps: Strong spring clamps are used to hold fabrics in place, especially when making curtains. Smaller clamps are used to hold fabrics, pleats, and bandings.

Cutting tools: Good-quality scissors and shears are a great investment. Choose the size and style that best fits your hand. Long shears are good for cutting widths of fabric. Use medium-length blades for cutting around curves and shapes. Small scissors are used for cutting details and corners, and nippers are handy at the sewing machine for clipping threads. Rotary cutters can be used for cutting banding and welt cord.

General hand tools: These are needed for making and installing window treatments. You will need a heavy-duty stapler and drill, plus an assortment of screwdrivers, a tack hammer, and an awl.

Iron: Use a general steam iron with a heavy sole plate. Professional workrooms will often have boiler irons, which generate steam evenly for long periods of time.

Measuring tools: Every workroom has rulers in many different lengths, from short pocket-size versions to yardsticks and 48-, 60-, and 72-inch-long (122, 152, and 183 cm) rulers and a carpenter's square. A good, sturdy tape measure is a must for measuring windows and finished drapery lengths. Look for heavy-duty metal tape measures in 12- and 25-foot (3.6 and 7.3 m) lengths. A soft tape measure is used for measuring bedding, pillows, and slipcovers and to determine drops and curves. Clear quilter's rulers are wonderful for cutting bandings and welt cord, marking inset trims, and measuring hems.

Workroom clamps are used to hold fabrics to the worktable, especially when making large curtains.

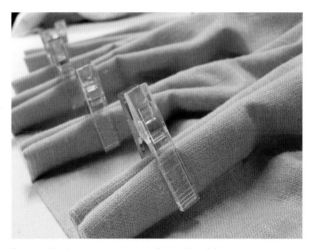

Small quilter's clamps are handy for holding fabrics.

Sewing machines: Use a good-quality machine that can sew multiple thicknesses. The most common stitch used is a straight stitch. Occasionally a zigzag stitch is used for finishing edges or making buttonholes. An overlock machine or serger is an excellent tool for joining fabrics and finishing edges.

FUNDAMENTAL TECHNIQUES

In this section you will learn the basic sewing skills that will be used over and over when making window treatments. You will learn how to cut and match pattern motifs and add hems, linings, trims, and other finishing touches. You will refer back to this section often.

working with fabrics

CUTTING

It is important to cut fabrics as straight and square as possible, but it can be a challenge because fabrics can shift and move. When making the initial cuts, add a few extra inches (7.6 cm) so that you will not come up short if a cut is uneven. This is called a "workroom allowance" or "tabling allowance" and is a common practice. There are several techniques for cutting, which are shared below. You will want to experiment to see what works best for the fabric at hand.

Pulling a Thread

Clip the selvage and separate one thread from the horizontal weave of the fabric and gently pull the thread to gather up the fabric.

Keep pulling until the thread breaks. Flatten out the fabric and cut along the line created by the pulled thread. When you get to the end of the line, find the end of the thread or choose another thread and keep pulling and cutting.

On some fabrics you can pull a thread and cut at the same time, holding the thread tight and keeping the blade of the scissors next to the thread. This takes a little practice but is a fast and fun way to cut fabrics square.

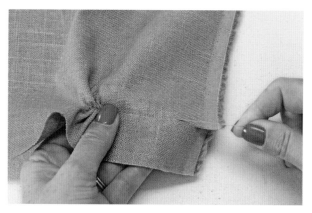

Clip the selvage and pull a thread.

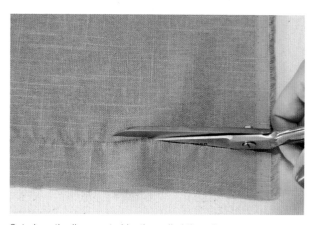

Cut along the line created by the pulled thread.

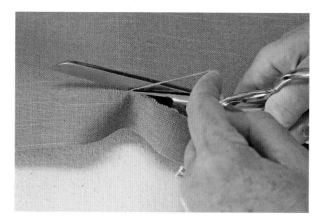

Pull a thread and hold it taut while you cut.

Folding and Cutting

Not all fabrics can be cut by pulling a thread. Another option is to fold the fabric over on itself, lining up the selvages to create a square, even fold at the cut length. Run the scissors into the fold and cut, or press a crease line as a mark. This can be an efficient way to roll out fabrics when cutting to a pattern repeat.

You can also use rulers and carpenter's squares to mark and cut fabrics. This is a good approach when fabrics are printed off-grain, so that you can work with the fabric face up and make slight adjustments if needed.

SEAMS

Fabrics are joined together with simple seams, sewn with a straight stitch. The size of the seam allowance depends on the selvage width or the pattern match. Do not cut off the selvages until you have determined how the fabric will be sewn.

After sewing, the selvages can then be trimmed to ½ inch (1.3 cm) from the stitch line. The seams can be pressed open or pressed to one side. A serged seam can be used for fabrics that fray or that will be unlined, and the seam pressed to one side.

An encased, French seam is used when the seam will be visible, such as with unlined curtains. To make a French seam, stitch or serge together the fabrics with wrong sides together. Turn the fabric along the seam with right sides together, press, and pin. Sew to the outside of the seam, encasing the seam.

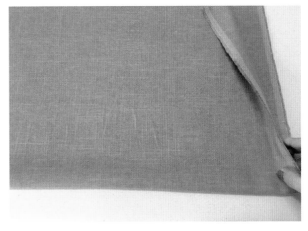

Fold the fabric so that the selvages are even on each side.

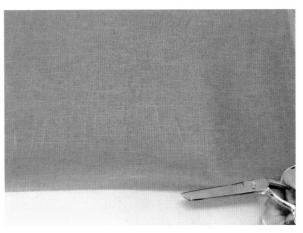

Cut along the fold.

Fold patterned fabrics to the length needed to match the pattern repeat and cut along the fold.

HEMMING

Hems are used along the side and bottom edges, and are usually folded over twice for extra body and to hide cut edges.

Hand sewing gives the best-quality finish. Press hems and pin. Set the pins at an angle and bury the points to prevent snags and picks. For hand sewing hems, use a strong thread like one suitable for hand quilting and long, sharp needles (darners) plus a pair of nippers and a thimble.

A slipstitch, running stitch, overcast stitch, or blanket stitch can all be used to sew hems. To make the hem less visible, catch only a tiny amount of the fabric with the needle and space the stitches evenly about ½ inch (1.3 cm) apart.

A machine-sewn blind stitch can also be used. Test the fabric first to make sure it will feed evenly. You will want to set the stitches so that the least amount of stitching shows. For some projects, a straight stitch can be used to finish the hems. This is a sturdy, practical finish for curtains that will be washed. Straight stitching can also be used as a decorative detail in a contrasting color.

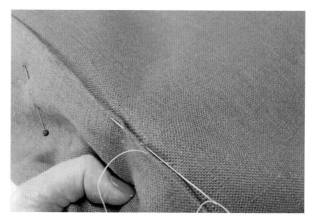

Use a slipstitch for an invisible hem from the front and back. The thread is hidden inside the fold.

Use a blanket stitch when the project is lined.

Use a blind hem attachment to finish hems by machine.

Fusible hemming tape can be used for a quick and easy finish. Test the fabric first to make sure the fabric can accept a hot iron, and that the tape doesn't show through to the front.

Side hems often have lining and even interlining included in the folds, which can make them thicker. They are not more difficult to sew, but the extra layers can cause take-up or puckering. Hand sewing is ideal for side hems, but they can also be finished by machine or with fusible products.

Fold a doubled hem and pin. Sew along the underside of the hem, stitching into the fold and into the lining only, and catching the face fabric about every 6 inches (15.2 cm), or a hand width apart, with a tiny stitch to the front. Keep the tension on the thread even and not too tight. You don't want dimples to show on the front! At the corners, use a ladder stitch for a neat and invisible finish.

Use a ladder stitch to close bottom corners on side hems. Pull the thread so the stitches are hidden.

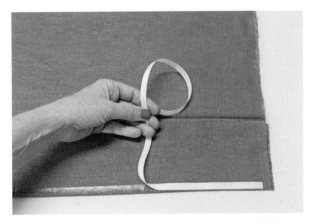

Press fusible hem tape to the top back edge of the hem fold. Fold over again and press to finish.

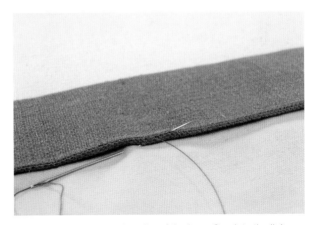

Hide the stitches under the edge of the hem. Sew into the lining but only catch the face fabric with a tiny stitch every 6 inches (15.2 cm).

MATCHING PATTERN MOTIFS

When working with patterned fabrics you will want to match the pattern at the seams, so the design will be consistent across the window treatment, and from one window in the room to another. Look at the fabric and find a repeating design, such as a flower, and measure.

When purchasing fabric, the pattern repeat is factored into the calculations. You will divide the cut length by the pattern repeat to determine the adjusted cut length.

For example, if you need 96-inch (244 cm) cuts for your project and the pattern repeat is 27 inches (68.6 cm), you will divide 96 by 27 for a result of 3.5. In order to have enough fabric for matching, round up to 4 repeats per cut. The adjusted cut length is 27 inches × 4 = 108 inches (274.3 cm).

There are different types of pattern repeats, from centered to offset designs. Most fabrics will have a pattern that matches straight across so that when you cut to a repeat, all the cuts will line up evenly. But there are some fabrics with a "drop repeat," where the motif does not match straight across from one selvage to the other. The pattern might drop half of a repeat, or even a whole repeat.

When using a drop repeat there will be some waste, as you adjust to match patterns. But with some planning, the waste is minimized. Plan your first cut, then drop down to make the next cut to match. If you were to make all the cuts the same, you will end up with an uneven match. When sewing multiple widths together, plan your first cuts and then the drop match cuts. For example, if you need three cuts, you will cut two exactly alike and then drop down to the matching motif and cut one more. You only waste one repeat.

Measure the pattern repeat from one flower to the next matching flower.

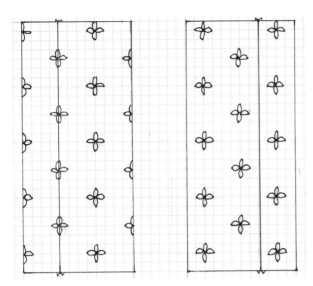

Examples of centered and offset pattern motifs matched with one and a half widths of fabric.

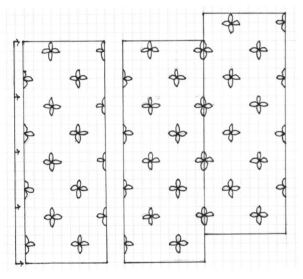

There are four repeats in this example of a drop repeat. You will come up short if you cut both pieces the same because the pattern doesn't line up across the width.

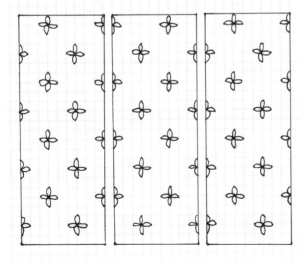

Three widths are cut to match a drop repeat with the center section using a different starting motif than the two outer cuts.

JOINING FABRICS AND MATCHING PATTERNS

After your fabric is cut, mark the direction of the pattern motif on each cut. Sometimes there will be an arrow on the selvage indicating the direction, but not all fabrics have this. You can mark with a pin at the bottom, or a piece of tape.

Two methods for matching patterns are shown using fusible tape or pins. Practice both techniques and use the best option for your project.

Matching with Fusible Tape

1 Place one piece of fabric face up. Fold under the selvage edge of the next piece of fabric to determine where the pattern will match. The match might be right at the edge of the selvage, or over into the design. (A) Once you find the match, press under the selvage so that it matches the other piece. (B)

2 Apply iron-on fusible tape along the edge, under the fold. (C) Remove the paper strip (D) and with both fabrics face up iron the fabrics together, matching the pattern and joining the fabrics with the fusible tape. (E)

3 Fold the fabrics face to face and stitch in the crease line. Cut off the excess selvage to ½ inch (1.3 cm). You can also serge the seam. Press the seam to one side.

With the fabrics face up, fold under the selvage on one piece to find where it matches.

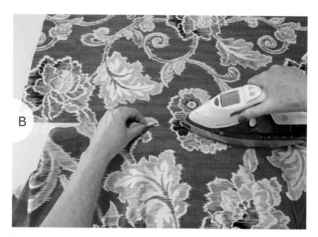

Press under the selvage to match.

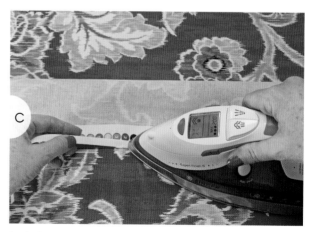

Apply fusible tape under the folded edge.

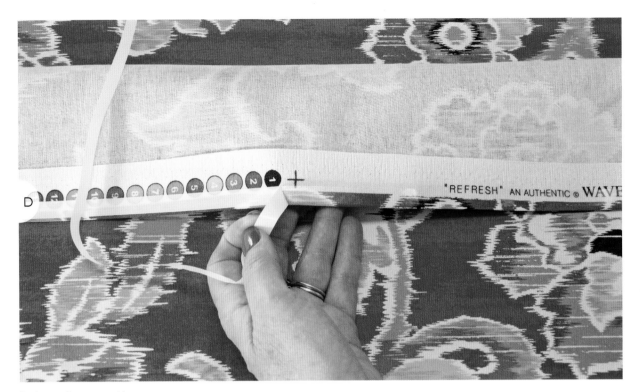

Peel away the paper strip.

Iron the fabrics together, melting the fusible tape and matching the pattern.

Matching with Pins

1 Place one piece of fabric face up and the other piece on top face down, with the patterns going in the same direction and the selvage edges lined up evenly. Fold over the selvage to find where the pattern matches and press a crease. **(A)**

2 Carefully stab pins through the crease, into the fabric below and back out, adding pins 3 to 4 inches (7.6 to 10.2 cm) apart. Continue down the entire edge. **(B)**

3 Fold the fabric over to show the crease line and stitch along the crease, removing pins as you sew. **(C)**

4 After the seam is sewn, cut the selvages to ½ inch (1.3 cm) and press the seams open, or press to one side, depending on your fabric and project. **(D)**

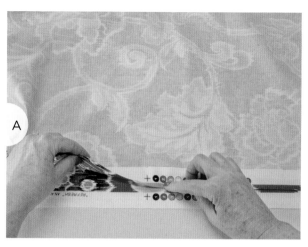

A

Fold over the selvage to find the match.

B

Pin into the crease, securing the two fabrics together where the pattern matches.

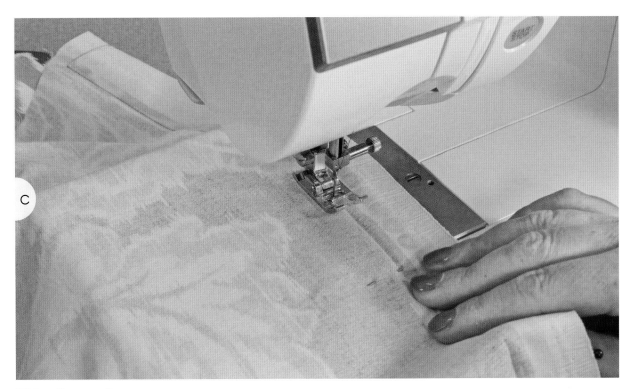

Stitch on the crease line

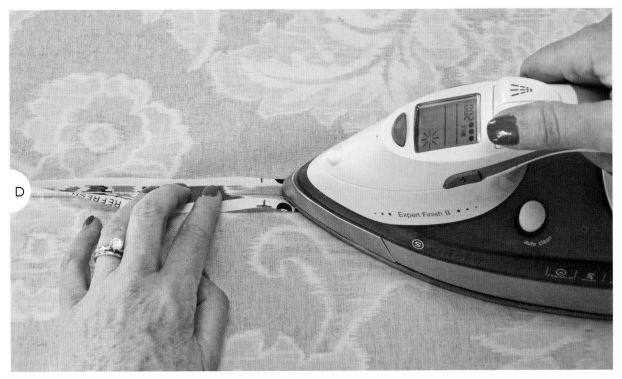

Press the seam open.

making covered welt cord

Welt cord (also called piping cord) is used in seams as a decorative detail and also strengthens and adds body to seams and edges. Welt cord comes in many different diameters, but for window treatments the most common size is ½ inch (1.3 cm) diameter or less.

Cover welt cord with fabric that is cut into strips. Cut on the bias or diagonal of the fabric if the cord will be sewn around shapes or curves.

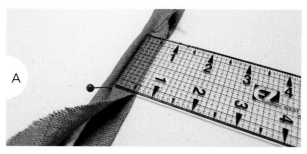

1 To determine the cut size, wrap the fabric around the cord, adding for the seam. The size will vary based on the thickness of the fabric and the diameter of the cord. **(A)**

2 Sew the strips together. Use a zipper foot or welt cord foot to sew the fabric around the welt cord. Do not sew too close to the cord. **(B)**

3 Sew the covered cord to the main fabric. **(C)**

4 Sew the front to the back, getting close to the welt cord. The last stitch line should be snug against the cord. **(D)** Admire your finished welt cord. **(E)**

understanding fullness

The term fullness describes the amount of extra fabric needed to create pleats or gathers in fabric in relation to the finished size. A common fullness ratio used in window treatments is to multiple two and a half times the rod, window, or finished width.

As you study the instructions, you will see the recommended fullness for different styles. Some window treatments require very little to no fullness. A flat, Roman shade doesn't require any fullness. The only extra fabric used is an allowance for hems. This style uses less fabric than a gathered or pleated shade.

In the illustration below, you can see the difference between two, two and a half, and three times fullness. Two times fullness is used for flat panel styles like grommet or tab-top curtains, two and a half times fullness gathers nicely for rod pocket or shirred and pleated curtains, and three times fullness is used for very generous, full pleated curtains.

The more fullness you use, the more fabric you will need. When calculating yardage, you may choose to go down to the lesser fullness to save fabric, or move up to the greater fullness if the windows are tall or more fabric is needed to achieve the desired results.

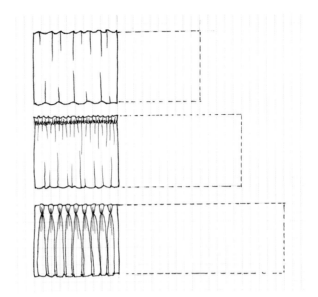

Examples of fullness.

cord safety

Cords on window treatments like curtains, shades, and blinds can pose a potential strangulation hazard to young children. According to the U.S. Consumer Product Safety Commission, corded window coverings are among the top five hidden hazards in American homes. This is especially important with older window coverings that may not meet the latest national standards for window cord safety.

WHY ARE CORDS DANGEROUS?

Children can become entangled in operating cords dangling on the side or front of the window covering and cords on the back of shades can be pulled away from the fabric, creating a loop.

SAFETY PRODUCTS AND STANDARDS

In the United States and other countries, safety standards are now in place for manufacturers, importers, and retailers to follow. The standards are created by a collaboration of industry organizations, government agencies, and consumer groups. Since the implementation of safety standards, there has been an increased awareness of cord safety and exciting, new product innovations.

On styles with vertical lift cords like Roman shades, cord shrouds and locks are used to control the distance that the cords can be pulled away from the window covering, lessening the size of the hazardous loop. Tension devices are used for operating systems that lift or traverse with a bead chain or cord loop, keeping it taut and anchored to the wall.

A tension device anchors the cord loop securely to the wall.

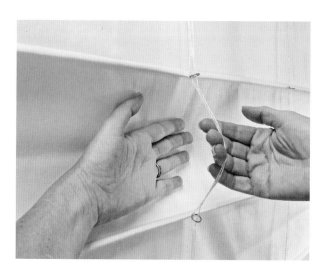

A cord shroud controls the size of the loop formed by the combination of cord and shade fabric. The shroud must be attached to the shade so that the loop stays within safety standards.

When installing new window treatments, be sure to follow the manufacturer's instructions and use the safety features and devices.

Window covering retailers, professional designers, decorators, workrooms, and window treatment installers should stay informed of new products and changes to national standards and educate clients about cord safety.

SAFETY COMES FIRST, DECORATING SECOND

It is always best practice to use cord-free window coverings. If you have old, outdated window coverings with cords, you should remove them or see if you can make them cord-free. Cords can be cut off and removed from traverse curtain rods and then easily operated by hand or with a baton. Soft shades can be retrofitted with cord shrouds, or simply set in a fixed position and the cords removed. Another practical step to ensure safety is to move all cribs, beds, furniture, or toys away from windows and window coverings.

EXAMPLES OF SAFE, CORD-FREE WINDOW COVERINGS

+ Grommet or tab-top curtains

+ Shutters

+ Pleated curtains with cord-free hardware

+ Curtains gathered on a rod

+ Spring roller shades

+ Top treatments like gathered valances, cornice boards, or swags

+ Shades and blinds with hand-lift options and no exposed cords

+ Stationary, non-operable soft shades

To retrofit a traverse rod, remove the cords and attach a baton to the master carrier.

Use the baton to open and close the curtains.

CURTAINS AND DRAPERIES

Can you imagine a world without curtains? They are one of the most popular styles of window treatments and also can serve as room dividers, backdrops, and privacy curtains. Add interlining and your curtains will insulate your windows, and with blackout linings you can control light. From sheer, short café curtains to long, luxurious silk ball gown style, every window in any room can be complemented with curtains and draperies.

MAKING A BASIC CURTAIN PANEL

All curtains are made in a similar way, with hems on the bottom, sides, and top. The top hem, also known as the "heading," is then finished to create a variety of styles. A gathered curtain may have a rod pocket or a gathering tape sewn at the top, while a pleated curtain has crisp buckram added to the heading.

Multiple widths of material are sewn together to achieve the fullness needed. When possible, try to line up the seams in the face fabric and linings to prevent shadowing when light shines through the fabric.

The term panel is used to describe any size curtain, from a single width to multiple widths. You can have one three-width panel, for example.

Basic steps are shown here so that they do not need to be repeated for other projects in this chapter. Once you know the basic steps, you are ready to make almost any style of curtain!

GETTING STARTED

Allow extra for the bottom hem and heading. The most common bottom hem size is 4 inches (10.2 cm) doubled (allow 8 inches [20.3 cm]). You can vary the hem size based on the project. Short curtains can have smaller doubled hems and extra-tall curtains can have larger hems.

Finished length + hem and heading allowance = cut length

WHAT YOU WILL NEED

+ decorator fabric
+ lining (and interlining)
+ drapery weights

YARDAGE REQUIREMENTS

You will need to determine how much fullness your project requires to determine yardage requirements. Refer to specific projects for detailed calculations.

MAKING A BASIC CURTAIN WITH LINING

1 Cut and prepare fabrics, joining widths if needed. Hem the bottom edge of the face fabric with a 4-inch (10.2 cm) doubled hem and for the lining use a 3-inch (7.6 cm) doubled hem. Secure a drapery weight at seams (see page 14). Finish hems using your preferred method. (See Hemming, page 20.)

2 Place the hemmed face fabric facedown, and cut off the selvage edges. Place the lining faceup over the back of the hemmed fabric, smoothing it out neatly and evenly with the bottom edge inset 1 inch (2.5 cm) along the bottom hemmed edge of the face fabric. (A) If multiple widths are sewn together, line up the face fabric and lining seams, if possible.

3 Cut the lining 3 inches (7.6 cm) less than the fabric along each side. Fold over 3 inches (7.6 cm) along the side, tucking the cut edge under to create a 1½-inch (3.8 cm) doubled side hem. Press lightly. (B) Add a drapery weight inside the fold of the hem at the bottom corners. Secure with pins. (C) Repeat for the other side. When using multiple widths, pin together the fabrics down the seams and across the top before moving over to continue making the curtain.

4 Finish the side hems by hand or machine sewing.

5 Measure from the bottom to the top, marking for the finished length, allowing extra fabric to finish the top as needed for the style you are making.

(continued)

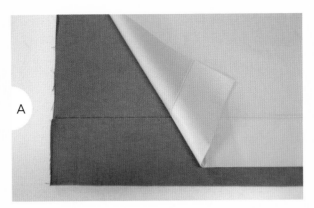

A

Place the lining faceup over the back of the curtain panel and inset 1 inch (2.5 cm) from the bottom. Trim away excess lining even with the side edges and tuck the cut edge under the side hem.

B

Fold a 1½-inch (3.8 cm) hem on each side and press.

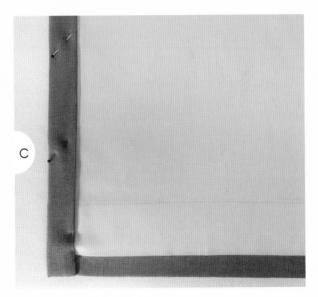

C

Use pins to secure the side hems.

MAKING A BASIC CURTAIN
WITH LINING AND INTERLINING

1 Cut and prepare the fabrics, joining widths if needed. Hem the bottom edge of the face fabric with a 4-inch (10.2 cm) doubled hem, and for the lining use a 3-inch (7.6 cm) doubled hem. Finish the hems using your preferred method. (See Hemming, page 20.)

2 Finish the bottom edge of the interlining by serging or with a zigzag stitch.

3 Place the hemmed face fabric facedown, and cut off the selvage edges. Place the interlining faceup over the back of the hemmed fabric, smoothing it out neatly and evenly with the bottom edge inset 2 inches (5 cm) along the bottom hemmed edge of the face fabric. If multiple widths are sewn together, line up the face fabric and interlining seams, if possible. Cut the interlining 1½ inches (3.8 cm) less than the fabric along each side.

4 Place the hemmed lining fabric faceup over the interlining with the bottom hem inset 1 inch (2.5 cm) along the bottom edge of the face fabric. Cut the lining 3 inches (7.6 cm) less than the fabric along each side. (A)

5 Fold over the face fabric along the sides to create a 1½-inch (3.8 cm) doubled hem, including the interlining in the fold and tucking the cut edge of the lining under the doubled side hem. Press lightly. Add a drapery weight to the bottom corners and at the seams. (See page 14.) Secure with pins. (B)

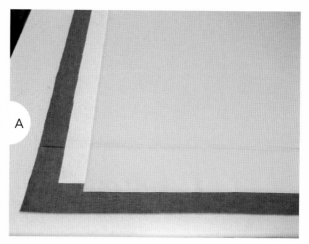

Along the sides of the curtain cut the interlining 1½ inches (3.8 cm) less than the face fabric, and the lining 3 inches (7.6 cm) less. When the side hem is folded over, the interlining will be included for a single fold

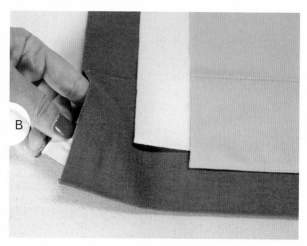

A drapery weight is tucked into the bottom of the side hem. Drapery weights are also added at the seams.

6 Finish the side hems by hand or machine sewing.

7 Measure from the bottom to the top, marking for the finished length, allowing extra fabric to finish the top as needed for the style you are making. (C)

Measure from the bottom to the top, folding over at the finished length.

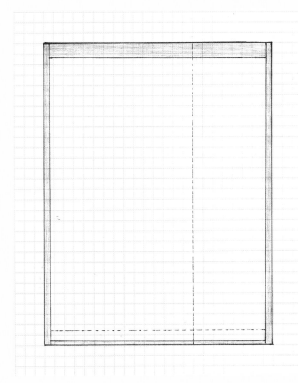

A typical curtain panel has a bottom hem, side hems, and a top heading. Vertical seams are lined up to prevent shadowing in sunlight.

Once you learn how to make the basic curtain panel, the possibilities are endless! This pretty drapery has a pleated heading and inset trim.

GROMMET CURTAIN

Grommet curtains are a popular yet uncomplicated style. The curtain panels are flat, but when a decorative pole is threaded through the grommets, a clean, serpentine shape is formed. Because very little sewing is required, this style is a good choice for less experienced curtain makers.

GETTING STARTED

Follow instructions for making a basic curtain. For the top heading, allow enough fabric for a double fold to the back. The amount can vary based on the diameter of the grommets. Generally, allow at least 1 inch (2.5 cm) above and below the inside edge of the grommets for the heading. For this project, a 4-inch (10.2 cm) double-fold heading was used.

Select a rod that is a smaller diameter than the grommets, so the curtain will slide easily. Plan to use grommets with an inside diameter of 30 to 40 percent more than the rod diameter if the curtain will be operable.

WHAT YOU WILL NEED

+ decorator fabric
+ lining
+ grommets
+ iron-on buckram
+ drapery weights
+ hardware for installation

YARDAGE REQUIREMENTS

If using a print fabric, additional fabric may be needed to match the pattern motif.

Face Fabric

Finished length + 16 inches (40.6 cm) for the bottom hem and top heading = cut length

Finished width × 2 fullness ÷ fabric width = number of widths per window (round up)

Cut length × number of widths ÷ 36 inches (91.4 cm) = number of yards (meters) needed

Lining

Finished length + 6 inches (15.2 cm) bottom hem = cut length

Cut length × number of widths ÷ 36 inches (91.4 cm) = number of yards (meters) needed

If possible, install the rod above the window and measure the finished width and length. Remember that the top of the rod is not the finished length—it is where the inside of the grommet sits on the rod. The top edge of the curtain will be above the rod. This is also important to remember if you are mounting close to the ceiling. Be sure to leave enough space above the rod for the top of the curtain.

Always plan for an even number of grommets so that the outside and inside edges both face in the same direction and toward the wall.

Measure the distance from the wall to the center of the pole. This is the "return." Measure the return at each end and in the center of the rod, because the window trim may jut out, making the center returns less than the outer returns.

(continued)

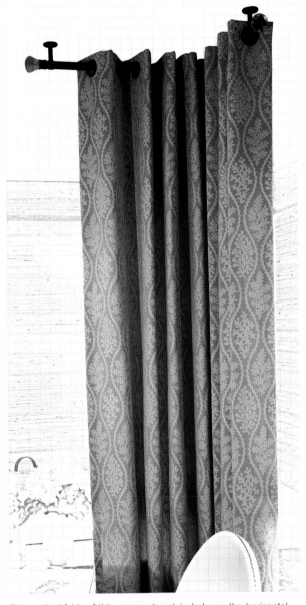

The vertical folds of this grommet curtain balance the horizontal lines of the windows and blinds. Ceiling-mounted hardware is a handsome feature and a clever solution.

MAKING A GROMMET CURTAIN

1 Follow instructions for making a basic curtain, measuring the length and turning over excess fabric at the top. For example, allow 8 inches (20.3 cm) extra for a 4-inch (10.2 cm) double-fold heading. Iron a crease to mark the finished length. Trim away excess lining even with the finished length.

2 Turn the curtain panel so that the heading is facing you, lining side up. Cut a piece of buckram 6 inches (15.2 cm) wider than the finished panel width. Press a double fold in the top heading and place the buckram inside the fold, folding over the excess on each end (this provides more body at each end). **(A)**

3 Secure the heading by using fusible hem tape or fabric glue under the folded edge. **(B)**

The curtain heading is folded and pressed. Buckram is used to add stability and create a crisp top edge.

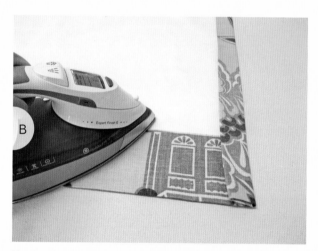

The heading is pressed. Fusible hem tape provides a temporary hold until the grommets are set.

4 Mark for the grommets. Begin by adding a mark for the outside return and the inside return. Measure between the marks and divide by an odd number. Generally, the grommets should be around 6 inches (15.2 cm) or less apart. (Do not space the grommets too far apart or the sections that fold behind the rod will not clear the wall.) (C)

5 Center a grommet over each mark and draw around the inside circumference of the grommet. (D)

(continued)

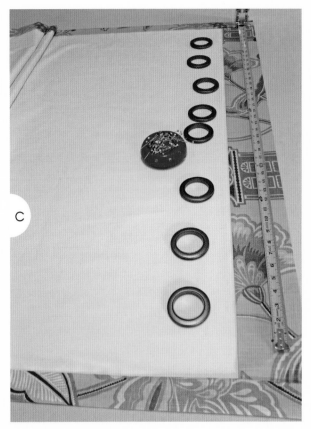

Pins mark the inside and outside returns. The measurement between the marks is then divided by seven for this one-width panel, which will have eight grommets.

Center a grommet over each mark and draw around the inside diameter.

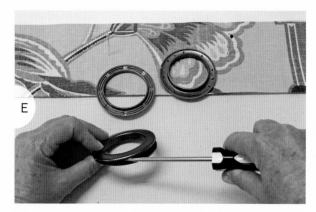

Pry apart plastic grommets with a flat screwdriver.

A staple is used in the center of each circle. This holds the heading together and makes cleanup easy!

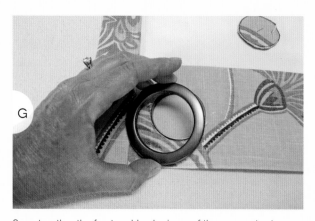

Snap together the front and back pieces of the grommet set. Glue can be added around the neck of the grommet for a more secure bond.

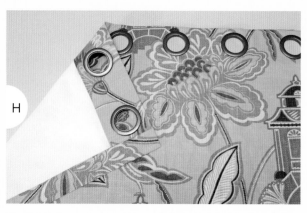

The finished grommet panel is ready to be installed on the window.

6 Separate the grommets into two pieces, front and back. (E)

7 Staple in the center of each circle. Cut one hole at a time. Cut slightly larger than the mark so the grommet will not be too snug. (F)

8 Place the front piece of the grommet through the hole and snap the pieces together. (If using metal grommets, a setting tool will need to be used.) Continue cutting holes and setting grommets across the heading. (G)

9 When all the grommets are set, the curtain is ready to install. Thread the rod through the grommets with the outside and inside edges turned toward the back. (H)

Note: When making multiple-width panels, it is important to place the seams in the spaces that go behind the rod. To do this, make a template of the grommet placement first, before cutting and joining fabrics. Mark for seams on the template and then use this to lay out your fabrics. You may need to trim away fabric off the leading edge or slightly adjust the grommet spacing.

The grommet curtain is installed on a smooth iron rod and opens and closes easily.

WAVE CURTAIN WITH CLIP–ON RINGS

This style of curtain has a wave or serpentine shape, minimal fullness, and a clean and uncluttered appearance. The look is similar to grommet curtains, but this version is installed with clip-on rings. Vertical stitching is used to hold the layers together, and provides a hidden spot for the clip-on rings.

GETTING STARTED

Buckram is used to hold the shape across the top. Just about any type of fabric is suitable for this style. If using a thin fabric, interlining can be added for extra body.

(continued)

WHAT YOU WILL NEED

+ decorator fabric
+ lining
+ iron-on buckram
+ drapery weights
+ iron-on fusing web
+ rings with attached clips and other hardware for installation

YARDAGE REQUIREMENTS

If using a print fabric, additional fabric may be needed to match the pattern motif.

FACE FABRIC

Finished length + 12 inches (30.5 cm) = cut length

Finished width × 2 fullness ÷ fabric width = number of widths per window (round up)

Cut length × number of widths ÷ 36 inches (91.4 cm) = number of yards (meters) needed

LINING

Finished length + 9 inches (22.9 cm) top and bottom hem = cut length

Cut length × number of widths ÷ 36 inches (91.4 cm) = number of yards (meters) needed

The wave curtain has a sleek, contemporary style.

MAKING A WAVE CURTAIN
WITH CLIP-ON RINGS

1 Follow instructions for making a basic curtain, adding lining and drapery weights at the side hems and seams. Measure from the bottom edge to the top, adding 4 inches (10.2 cm) to the finished length. Mark and cut off any excess fabric.

2 Turn the curtain panel so that the heading is facing you, lining side up. Cut a piece of iron-on buckram 7 inches (17.8 cm) wider than the finished panel width. Iron the buckram to the back of the fabric, even with the top edge and folding over 3½ inches (8.9 cm) of extra buckram at each end. (A)

3 Fold over and press the fabric with the buckram attached, so that the top edge of the buckram is even with the finished length. (B)

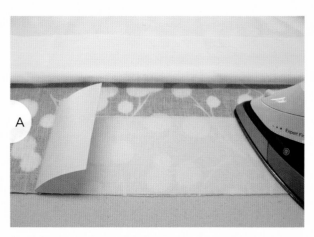

Attach iron-on buckram to the back top edge.

Fold over the buckram and fabric and press.

4 Fold under the lining across the reverse side of the curtain and, using one of the rings with clips attached, measure the distance between the ring and where it clips to the lining. For this curtain the lining will need to be 1 inch (2.5 cm) less than the top edge of the curtain to hide the clips. (C)

5 Press the lining evenly across the top. Unfold and cut off excess fabric past the crease so that it will be even with the bottom edge of the buckram that is at the top of the curtain. On this curtain, 3 inches (7.6 cm) of lining is folded under at the top, to line up evenly with the 4-inch (10.2 cm) buckram, leaving a 1-inch (2.5 cm) reveal of face fabric across the reverse side.

6 Fold and press the side hems. Sew around the corners, and finish the side hems. The curtain is ready to be marked and tacked.

7 Measure and mark for the placement of the clip-on rings. To create a return to the wall, begin with your first mark based on the size of the return on your hardware. For the leading edge, mark next to the side hem. Measure in between the two marks to create spacing that is 5 to 6 inches (12.5 to 15.2 cm) apart. (D)

(continued)

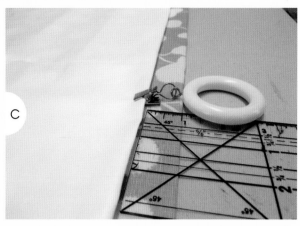

C

Use a clip-on ring to determine the placement of the lining. The clip will be hidden behind the top of the curtain.

D

The first mark is inset from the edge, for the return. Use an erasable marker to draw two vertical lines, wide enough for the clips.

8 At each mark, draw two vertical lines ¾ inch (1.8 cm) apart and ¾ inch (1.8 cm) high on the back of the lining, using an erasable or disappearing marker. This will be where each ring will be clipped.

9 Pin together the layers of fabric and buckram between the marks to hold the lining in place. (E)

Pin between the marks to hold all the layers together.

10 Use iron-on fusing web to attach the lining to the back of the curtain between the marks. (F)

11 Straight stitch on the vertical marks, sewing through all the layers, making two rows of stitching. Use a thread that matches the face fabric. This will create the space where the rings will be clipped.

12 Clip rings to the back of the curtain, between the stitch lines, and install on a pole rod.

Use iron-on fusing web in the spaces between the marks.

The wave curtain creates pretty columns of fabric when pushed open.

When pulled closed, the curtain has a less pronounced wave shape.

GATHERED CURTAIN STYLES

Gathered fabric curtains add texture and softness to the window. This can be achieved by sewing a sleeve or pocket across the top and shirring onto a rod or with shirring or gathering tape that has pull-cords for gathering.

ROD POCKET WITH TIEBACKS

Who doesn't love a pretty, gathered curtain with tiebacks? This style is suitable for bedrooms, kitchens, and dormer windows and can even be used for travel trailers! Short lengths work well over radiators or window seats for a feminine, cottage look. Floor-length tieback curtains can be an elegant addition to formal rooms.

GETTING STARTED

Follow the instructions for making a basic curtain. For the top heading, allow enough fabric for a double fold to the back that is large enough to create a pocket for the rod, and extra above the rod for the top ruffle. The amount can vary based on the style of hardware and thickness of the fabric.

Use light- to medium-weight fabric that will gather and drape with ease. Lining is optional. This is the perfect style for sheer and unlined fabrics. If you would like curtains that can be put in the washer and dryer, this is a good choice if the fabrics are washable and colorfast. Prewash all fabrics before sewing.

Determine the size of the rod pocket by wrapping fabric with lining around the rod and pinning together, leaving enough space for the fabric to move easily. The size of the top ruffle should be 1 to 3 inches (2.5 to 7.6 cm).

WHAT YOU WILL NEED

+ decorator fabric
+ lining
+ drapery weights
+ fusible fleece
+ welt cord
+ hardware for installation

YARDAGE REQUIREMENTS

If using a print fabric, additional fabric may be needed to match the pattern motif.

FACE FABRIC

Finished length + 8 inches (20.3 cm) bottom hem + allowance for rod pocket and top ruffle = cut length

Finished width × 2.5 fullness ÷ fabric width = number of widths per window (round up)

Cut length × number of widths ÷ 36 inches (91.4 cm) = number of yards (meters) needed

LINING

Finished length + 6 inches (15.2 cm) bottom hem + allowance for rod pocket and top ruffle = cut length

Cut length × number of widths ÷ 36 inches (91.4 cm) = number of yards (meters) needed

Gathered curtains with tiebacks are a good choice for dormer and inset windows.

For this window the curtains meet in the middle and the rod is hidden, so a white adjustable utility rod is a good choice. A decorative pole rod can also be used. Install the rod above the window and measure the finished length, adding for the top ruffle above the rod. If space is limited, this style can be made with just the rod pocket, and no ruffle at the top.

The tiebacks are made in a curved shape to hold the fabric without the tieback being crushed. Fusible fleece is added for extra body and softness.

(continued)

MAKING A ROD POCKET WITH TIEBACKS

1 Follow instructions for making a basic curtain, allowing extra fabric for a double-fold heading large enough for the rod pocket and top ruffle.

For example, this curtain has a 1½-inch (3.8 cm) rod pocket and a 2-inch (5 cm) top ruffle, which equals 3½ inches (8.9 cm). To create the double fold, allow 7 inches (17.8 cm).

2 With the panel facedown, fold and press the double-fold heading. Measure and mark for the top ruffle. Pin and sew across the bottom edge and along the mark.

3 Determine the size of the tiebacks by gathering one curtain panel to the finished width and cinching with a soft tape measure, or installing the finished curtain and cutting sample tiebacks from muslin to visualize the finished curtain shape. Generally, tiebacks will be at least 18 inches (45.7 cm) long for single-width panels. Add 4 to 6 inches (10.2 to 15.2 cm) for wider windows with panels using more widths of material. The finished size is based on the look you are trying to achieve.

Note: When using tiebacks, the leading edge will be pulled up. This is a pretty detail but it can show the lining if the curtain is tied back tightly. To make a straight hem, drape a cord on the window, tied back like the curtain will be, and then measure the cord. The length of the cord will be the finished length for the leading edge. The bottom of the curtain panel will angle slightly back to the return edge. In other words, the front edge will be longer, but when the curtain is tied back and dressed, it will all be even at the window.

Double fold the top heading, measure, and mark the top ruffle. Pin across the mark.

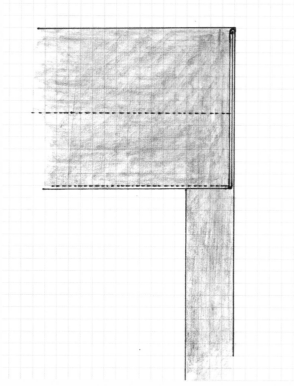

Sew along the bottom edge and inset from the top, creating the rod pocket and top ruffle.

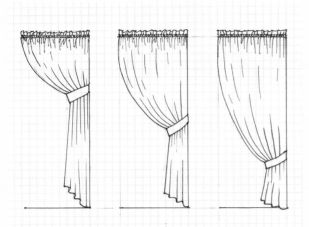

The placement of the tieback can change the look

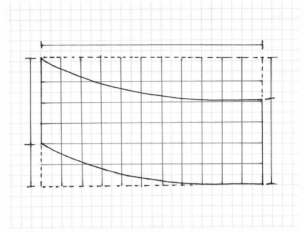

Draw the tieback pattern to scale on paper. This is for half the tieback. In this example, each red square is 1 inch (2.5 cm).

4 Make a pattern for the tieback using the illustration as a guide. Adjust the size for your project.

5 Place the pattern on the fabric, lining it up so that it is on the straight-of-grain. Measure and mark for a ½-inch (1.3 cm) seam allowance around the entire pattern. Cut this first piece and then use this to cut the other pieces. (A)

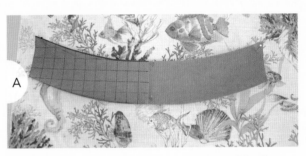

Place the pattern on the fabric and cut the shape, adding for a seam allowance.

6 When working with pattern motifs, you can feature a design on the tieback. Place the motif near the center right on the right tieback, and the center left on the left tieback.

7 Cut one each for each tieback: face fabric, lining fabric, and fusible fleece. The reverse side can be the same fabric or a plain lining. Cover enough welt cord to go around the edges. (See page 28.) (B)

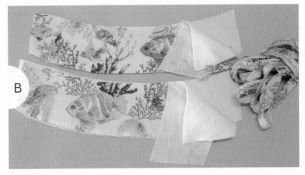

Fronts, backs, fusible fleece, and covered welt cord are ready to sew.

(continued)

8 Iron the face piece to the fusible fleece. Sew the welt cord around the edges. Pin the lining and face piece together, face-to-face, and sew close to the welt cord. Leave an opening for turning right sides out. Turn and press. Close the opening by hand stitching.

9 Sew rings on each end, insetting the ring on the front edge so that it is hidden. (C)

10 To install the curtains, insert the rod inside the rod pocket and push the fabric into gathers. Hang at the window. Straighten the curtain fabric and top ruffle and arrange the gathering evenly. (D)

11 Install small cup hooks into the wall at each side for the tiebacks. Wrap the tiebacks around the curtain panels and hook the rings over the cup hooks. Make sure the tiebacks are hanging at the same angle. Using your hands, smooth and fold the fabric so it falls in even, soft folds behind the tiebacks. (E)

Sew rings on each end.

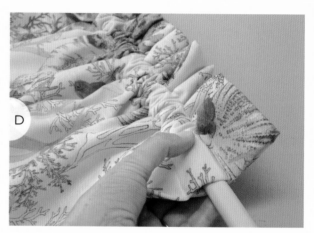

Slide the rod into the pocket below the top ruffle. Gather the fabric onto the rod.

Dress the fabric so the curtain falls into even folds behind the tieback.

SHIRRING TAPE

This version of a gathered curtain is made with shirring or gathering tape, which is sewn to the back of the curtain panel. Cords within the tape are pulled to create neat gathers.

GETTING STARTED

There are many different types of shirring tape, from a narrow tape with one cord to a wide tape with four cords. There are specialty tapes with smocking and other designs.

The tape is sewn to the back of the heading. Before pulling the cords, tie them securely at each end to prevent them from pulling out of the tape. For large curtains you can tie one end of the cords to a doorknob or table leg for support.

One of the great things about using shirring tape is that it is adjustable. If you leave the cords in place you can untie them to flatten the curtain panel for cleaning or adjusting for a different size. If you choose to leave the cords, sew a small pocket on the back of the curtain to store them.

(continued)

WHAT YOU WILL NEED

+ decorator fabric
+ lining
+ shirring tape
+ drapery weights
+ drapery pins and hardware for installation

YARDAGE REQUIREMENTS

If using a print fabric, additional fabric may be needed to match the pattern motif.

FACE FABRIC

Finished length + 8 inches (20.3 cm) bottom hem + allowance for top heading = cut length

Finished width × 2.5 fullness ÷ fabric width = number of widths per window (round up)

Cut length × number of widths ÷ 36 inches (91.4 cm) = number of yards (meters) needed

LINING

Finished length + 6 inches (15.2 cm) bottom hem = cut length

Cut length × number of widths ÷ 36 inches (91.4 cm) = number of yards (meters) needed

Shirring tape is used to create the gathered top on these floor-length curtains.

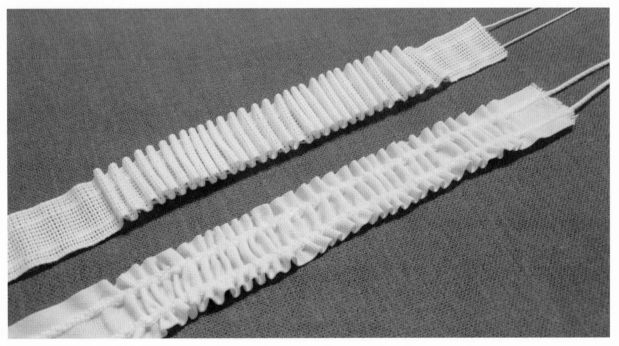

Two common styles of shirring tape used to create pencil pleats or simple gathering.

MAKING A SHIRRING TAPE CURTAIN

1 Follow instructions for making a basic curtain. For the top heading, allow enough fabric for a single fold to the back. The amount can vary based on the style of tape and the effect you would like to achieve. Cut away extra fabric.

2 Pin the shirring tape to the back, covering the cut edge of the face fabric. Sew each side and between the cords of the tape, using a matching thread. (A)

3 Tie off the cords securely on each end and pull up to the desired size. (B)

4 Insert drapery pins into the shirred tape on the back, spacing them 4 to 5 inches (10.2 to 12.7 cm) apart. (C)

5 Install and dress the drapery at the window. (See Installing Window Treatments, pages 109–122.)

(continued)

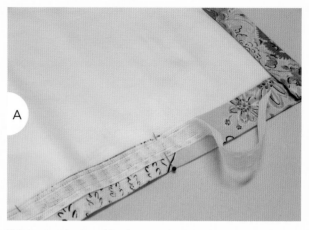

Shirring tape is pinned in place, ready to sew.

Pull the cords to create even gathers and tie off at the finished width.

Stab drapery pin hooks into the tape, making sure they do not stick through to the front. Insert the pin hooks into the ring eyelet.

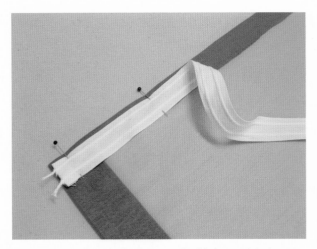

For a simple, gathered top edge, turn the fabric over 1 inch (2.5 cm) and cover the cut edge with the tape. Pin in place and sew the tape on each side and down the center.

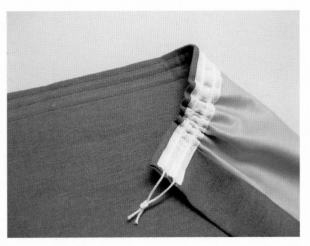

Pull the cords, gathering the fabric across the top.

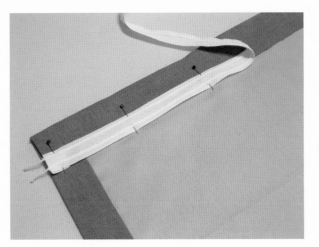

To make a ruffled heading, allow for additional fabric above where the tape is sewn. On this panel, 2½ inches (6.4 cm) extra is folded over.

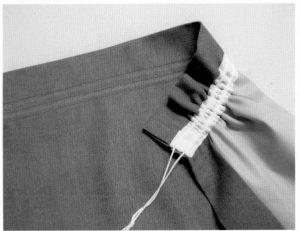

Pull the cords and the ruffle stands above the tape.

PLEATED CURTAIN STYLES

Pleated curtains or draperies are a timeless, classic window fashion that will never go out of style. There are many styles of pleats, which are sewn across the top of the fabric panel with even spacing. Pleated curtains can be traditional and formal in appearance, or cute and casual, depending on the fabrics used. They can be unlined, lined, or interlined. There are so many options!

A stiffener such as buckram or crinoline can be folded into the heading to help the pleats keep their shape. This is especially important for operable curtains, but you can also make pleated curtains without buckram.

There are two ways to add buckram to the top heading of the curtain: a double fold of fabric with the buckram included, or a single fold of fabric, which is known as the "low-bulk" method. Both options are shown and work equally well for pleated curtains. Use the double-fold heading if buckram is omitted.

To make curtains from sheer fabric without lining, reverse the steps by making the double fold of fabric with the buckram first, then measuring the length plus a hem allowance, cutting off excess fabric, finishing the bottom hem, and then finishing the side hems last.

Pleated curtains can be made to fit the window so that they can be drawn open and closed, and installed on traversing hardware or decorative poles with rings. They can also be purely decorative, pleated and hung on each side of the window in a fixed position. The beauty of fabric panels alone on each side of the window can be a great design choice, and curtains are a lovely complement over blinds or shutters, or under top treatments.

Goblet pleats dress the top of this curtain.

To create pleats, fullness is figured into the fabric calculations. The most common fullness ratio for pleated curtains is two and a half times, but this can vary based on the style of pleats and by using more or less fullness.

When planning pleated curtains it looks best to raise the hardware above the window and extend it at least a few inches on each side if room allows. You must also consider "stack-back," which is the space taken up by the drapery when it is drawn open. If there isn't enough room to extend the hardware past the window and onto the wall, you will have more of the curtain covering the window glass when it is opened.

UNDERSTANDING PLEATS AND SPACES

Before you calculate the pleats and spaces, you must know what type of hardware will be used, and whether the curtains will be one-way or two-way draw (also known as a split draw). A one-way draw is typical for a sliding door, with a large curtain panel opening to one side. A two-way draw has a pair of curtain panels, one on each side, and closes to the center.

Some curtain rods, known as "traverse rods," operate with a cord or baton, and the curtain hangs from small carriers that slide back and forth. You can also use simple decorative pole rods in wood or metal with rings that slide onto the pole. The rings will have small eyelets for attaching the curtain with pin hooks or clips.

To calculate pleats and spaces, you must know whether your hardware has an "overlap." The overlap is made up of two sturdy "master carriers" at the center that allow the curtain panels to close neatly without a light gap. Most traverse rods will have an overlap master carrier. The overlap size is normally 3½ inches (8.9 cm) and is included in the calculations for this style.

Here is a simple way to understand how pleats and spaces are figured. When you look at a pleated curtain, the flat areas or spaces between the pleats will cover the rod. The excess fabric or fullness beyond what is needed to cover the rod is then evenly divided into pleats.

(continued)

Buckram is used to create a crisp pleat.

This rod has overlapping master carriers. The curtains will overlap in the center.

GETTING STARTED

When making multiple-width panels, it is important to place the seams to the back of a pleat or to the side of a space, so it is less obvious, and never within a pleat. It is acceptable to adjust the size of your pleats slightly so that you can manage seams, while keeping the spaces even. For example, if you have a three-width panel with two seams, you may have 5-inch (12.7 cm) pleats on the first width, 4¾-inch (12.1 cm) pleats on the next width, and 5-inch (12.7 cm) pleats on the third width while keeping the spaces all the same. You may want to make a pleating template before you cut and sew fabrics so that you can plan the seam placement.

WHAT YOU WILL NEED

+ decorator fabric
+ lining
+ buckram

+ drapery weights
+ pin hooks
+ hardware for installation

YARDAGE REQUIREMENTS

FACE FABRIC

Finished length + 16 inches (40.6 cm) if using the double-fold heading or + 12 inches (30.5 cm) for the low-bulk heading = cut length

Finished width × 2.5 fullness ÷ fabric width = number of widths per window (round up)

Cut length × number of widths ÷ 36 inches (91.4 cm) = number of yards (meters) needed

If using a print fabric, additional fabric may be needed to match the pattern motif.

FACE FABRIC WITH PATTERN REPEATS

Finished length + 16 inches (40.6 cm) if using the double-fold heading or + 12 inches (30.5 cm) for the low-bulk heading ÷ the pattern repeat = number of pattern repeats for each cut

Pattern repeat × number of repeats = cut length

Finished width × 2.5 fullness ÷ fabric width = number of widths per window (round up)

Cut length × number of widths ÷ 36 inches (91.4 cm) = number of yards (meters) needed

LINING

Finished length + 6 inches (15.2 cm) if using the double-fold heading or + 9 inches (22.9 cm) if using the low-bulk heading = cut length

Cut length × number of widths ÷ 36 inches (91.4 cm) = number of yards (meters) needed

(continued)

Making a Double-Fold Heading

1 Follow instructions for making a basic curtain, adding lining and drapery weights at the side hems and seams. Measure from the bottom edge to the top, folding over the extra fabric and pressing a crease at the finished length. Cut off any excess fabric, leaving 8 inches (20.3 cm) folded over. **(A)**

2 Turn the curtain panel so that the heading is facing you, lining side up. Cut a piece of buckram 7 inches (17.8 cm) more than the finished panel width. Press a double fold in the top heading and place the buckram inside the fold, folding over the 3½ inches (8.9 cm) of extra buckram on each end (this provides more body for the overlap and return). **(B)** You can finish the heading with the side hems under or on top of the double fold. Either way is correct. **(C)**

3 Secure the heading with pins. You can use iron-on fusing web or fabric glue under the heading, but it isn't required because sewing the pleats will hold the layers together.

4 Sew around the corners, and finish the side hems. The curtain is ready to be pleated.

Cut off excess fabric, leaving 8 inches (20.3 cm) for the heading.

Fold the buckram over on each end for added body at the overlap and return areas.

Buckram is included inside the double-fold heading.

Making a Low-Bulk Heading

1 Follow instructions for making a basic curtain, adding lining and drapery weights at the side hems and seams. Measure from the bottom edge to the top, adding 4 inches (10.2 cm) to the finished length. Mark and cut off any excess fabric.

2 Turn the curtain panel so that the heading is facing you, lining side up. Cut a piece of iron-on buckram 7 inches (17.8 cm) wider than the finished panel width. Iron the buckram to the back of the fabric, even with the top edge and folding over 3½ inches (8.9 cm) of extra buckram at each end. (A)

3 Fold over and press the fabric with the buckram attached, so that the top edge of the buckram is even with the finished length.

4 Measure and cut off the lining 3½ inches (8.9 cm) longer than the finished length. (B)

5 Fold under the lining so that there is a ½-inch (1.3 cm) reveal of the face fabric at the top. Press the lining so that it is neat and flat. The bottom cut edge of the lining should be even with the bottom of the buckram. (C)

(continued)

Use fusible buckram for a low-bulk heading.

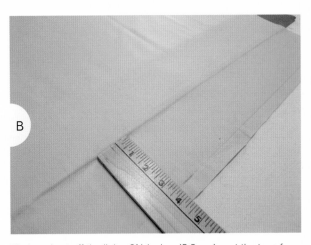
Mark and cut off the lining 3½ inches (8.9 cm) past the top of the curtain.

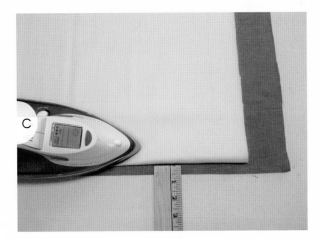
Fold under the lining ½ inch (1.3 cm) down from the top edge.

6 Secure the lining to the back of the heading with iron-on fusing web. (D)

7 Fold and press the side hems over the buckram heading. (E)

8 Sew around the corners, and finish the side hems. The curtain is ready to be pleated.

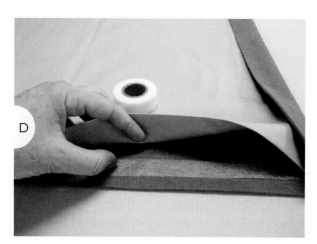

Attach the lining to the back with iron-on fusing web.

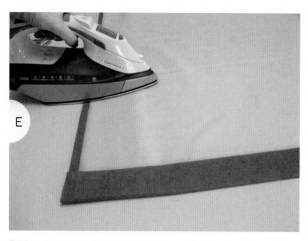

Fold and press the side hems and across the top.

Calculating Pleats and Spaces

To begin, answer these questions:

1. What type of hardware am I using?
   + Traverse rod
   + Decorative pole with rings (wood or metal)

2. How will it traverse?
   + Two-way draw from the center
   + One-way to the left or right only

Before you begin calculating pleats and spaces you will need to know the finished rod measurement, the size of the overlap master carrier (if using a traverse rod), and the projection of the hardware or "return." Make copies of the calculations on the following pages to use as worksheets, filling out the information for your specific project.

The following list shows the average number of pleats per width of material, based on a curtain using two and a half times fullness. Use this as a guideline as you work on your calculations.

1 width = 5 pleats
1½ widths = 7 pleats
2 widths = 10 pleats
2½ widths = 12 or 13 pleats
3 widths = 15 pleats
3½ widths = 17 or 18 pleats

Spaces between the pleats should be 3½ to 4 inches (8.9 to 10.2 cm) and each pleat will use 4½ to 6 inches (11.5 to 15.2 cm) of fabric.

Making a Traverse Curtain with Two-Way Draw

Two curtain panels will be pleated to fit the right and left sides of the rod plus overlap in the center and return to the wall.

Width of rod from outer edges = _____ + _____ overlap size + _____ return (there are two returns on this rod so double the measurement) = _____ ÷ 2 = _____ finished size of each curtain panel. After the pleats are sewn in, each panel will need to measure to this finished size.

PLEATS

Measure across one flat, unpleated panel = _____ - _____ finished size = _____ amount used for pleats. Divide by the number of pleats (based on the average of 5 pleats per width of material) = _____ size of each pleat

SPACES

Measure across the flat, unpleated panel = _____ - 3½ -inch (8.9 cm) overlap - _____ returns - _____ amount used for pleats. Divided by the number of spaces (one less than the number of pleats) = _____ size of each space

Making a Traverse Curtain with One-Way Draw

One curtain panel will be pleated to fit across the front of the rod plus a return to the wall on one side.

Width of rod from outer edges = _____ + _____ return = _____ finished size. After the pleats are sewn in, each panel will need to measure to this finished size.

PLEATS

Measure across the flat, unpleated panel = _____ - _____ finished size = _____ amount used for pleats. Divide by the number of pleats (based on the average of 5 pleats per width of material) = _____ size of each pleat

SPACES

Measure across the flat, unpleated panel = _____ - _____ return - _____ amount used for pleats. Divide by the number of spaces (one less than the number of pleats) = _____ of each space

(continued)

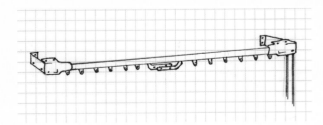

Two-way draw traverse rod.

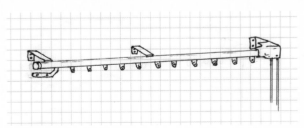

One-way draw traverse rod.

Making a Curtain for a Decorative Pole Rod with Rings and Two-Way Draw

Two drapery panels will be pleated to fit the right and left sides of the rod and meet in the center. There isn't an overlap carrier. Extra width is added for ease, or "spring back," on this style of rod.

Width of rod the curtain will cover (do not include finials) = _____ + 2 inches (5 cm) for ease + _____ return (there are two returns on this rod so double the measurement) ÷ 2 = _____ finished size of each curtain panel. After the pleats are sewn in, each panel will need to measure to this finished size.

PLEATS

Measure across the flat, unpleated panel = _____ - finished size = _____ amount used for pleats. Divide by the number of pleats (based on the average of 5 pleats per width of fabric) = _____ size of each pleat

SPACES

Measure across the flat, unpleated panel = _____ - 2 inches (5 cm) for ease - _____ returns - _____ amount used for pleats. Divide by the number of spaces (one less than the number of pleats) = _____ size of each space

Making a Curtain for a Decorative Pole Rod with Rings and One-Way Draw

One drapery panel will be pleated to fit across the front of the rod plus returns to the wall on one side.

Width of rod the curtain will cover (do not include finials) = _____ + 2 inches (5 cm) for ease + _____ return = _____ finished size. After the pleats are sewn in, the curtain panel will need to measure to this finished size.

PLEATS

Measure across the flat, unpleated panel = _____ - size that it needs to be finished after pleating = _____ divided by the number of pleats (based on the average of 5 pleats per width of fabric) = _____ size of each pleat

SPACES

Measure across the flat, unpleated panel = _____ - 2 inches (5 cm) for ease - _____ return - _____ amount used for pleats. Divide by the number of spaces (one less than the number of pleats) = _____ size of each space

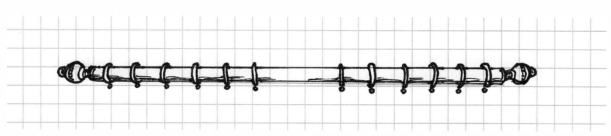

An example of a decorative pole rod with rings.

SEWING PLEATS

1 Use pins to mark the pleats and spaces. **(A)**

2 Sew a vertical seam from the top to the bottom of the heading. To keep the pleats even at the top, place the pleat under the presser foot and turn the hand wheel so that the needle is inserted into the pleat ½ inch (1.3 cm) down from the top, backstitch, and then sew. This will keep the layers from shifting. Sew 4 inches (10.2 cm) from the top to the bottom. When you are at the base of the pleat, backstitch again. **(B)**

3 After the pleats are sewn, measure to check the finished width. If it is not accurate you can adjust the width by taking out a few pleats and sewing again. Don't stress over fractions; it will not be noticeable when the curtain is hanging! **(C)**

(continued)

Pin together the pleats across the heading.

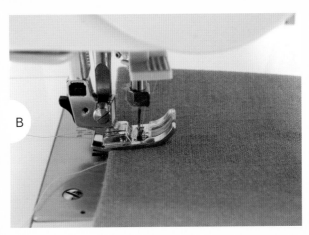

Seat the needle down into the fabric ½ inch (1.3 cm) from the top, then backstitch and continue sewing to the bottom of the heading.

Check the measurement after the pleats are sewn.

Different Styles of Pleats

A variety of pleat styles can be created by tacking with a needle and thread at the top, bottom, or center of the pleat. Use a long needle and two strands of heavy thread. Knot the thread and start by stabbing the needle inside one of the folds and out the side; this will hide the knot on the inside. Continue stitching to form one of the pleats shown at right and on page 71. When the pleat stitching is finished, stitch a knot and stab the needle into a thick area and out, pulling the knot into the fabric and trimming the thread.

FRENCH

The French pleat, also known as a pinch pleat, is divided into three sections, or "fingers." Pinch the pleat together and stitch at the base of the pleat. If using buckram, you will find it easier to stitch below the buckram. You can also stitch together at the top. This is optional. A two-finger French pleat can also be made using the same technique.

GOBLET

The pleat is tacked at the bottom like a French pleat, and then opened up and rounded at the top. To keep the rounded shape, foam or batting can be stuffed into the pleat.

Stab the needle through the thickness of the pleat and then trim away the excess thread.

French pleat.

Goblet pleat.

EURO

The pleat is divided into two or three sections and tacked at the top only by stab stitching from one side to the other, or by whipstitching the top edge to hold the folds together.

CARTRIDGE

The pleat has a simple, rounded shape and is not pinched or folded into sections. Stuff the pleats with rolled-up buckram or foam. Pipe insulation found in the plumbing department of the hardware store makes a great stuffing for cartridge pleats.

BUTTERFLY

The pleat is divided into two equal sections and tacked 2 inches (5 cm) down from the top, in the center of the heading.

Euro pleat.

Cartridge pleat.

Butterfly pleat.

SHADES AND BLINDS

There are many styles of shades: Roman, balloon, London, and more. Even though they have completely different looks, they all share one similarity. Shades operate vertically, raised up and lowered down, instead of traversing across the window like curtains. This offers more design options for your windows.

Shades and blinds are commonly paired with curtains for complete coverage of the window. A superior window covering for insulating the window and because they can be made with a small projection, they are a good choice for inside mounting and layering.

BASIC ROMAN SHADE

Roman shades are made from flat panels of fabric with rings sewn to the back in columns. Cord is threaded through the rings and when it is pulled, the fabric is lifted into even, horizontal folds. Choose stable home décor fabrics that do not stretch and preshrink fabrics by pressing with a steam iron prior to cutting and sewing. Roman shades can be functional and lifted up and down, but because they require cords you will want to familiarize yourself with important cord safety information found on pages 30–31. Best practice is to use only cord-free window treatments in homes with small children. Shades made today use safety products and cord shrouds to control hazardous cord loops.

Shade rings are available in metal or plastic. They all perform the same so you can select the style you prefer. If using plastic rings, make sure they are UV stable and designed for use on window treatments.

Nylon lift cord is available in different diameters such as 0.9 mm or 1.4 mm. Some shade systems require a specific size of cord. You can also purchase nylon-braided cord (also called "line") in the cord and rope aisle of your local home improvement store.

To meet safety standards, special products such a cord shrouds and RingLocks are used on the back of the shade to control how far the cord can be pulled away from the fabric, making it safer because the size of the combined loop of fabric and cord is minimized. Most cord control products are interchangeable with different lift systems but check with the supplier first to see if there are special requirements. You will see different options used for the projects in this section.

The basic, flat Roman shade is simple in style, and simple to make.

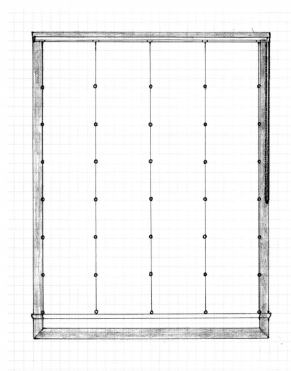

Back view of a basic Roman shade. Cord is threaded through columns of rings and into the lifting system.

GETTING STARTED

There are a wide variety of systems used for operating blinds and shades, from tracks with interior spools to roller tubes with a clutch, spring, or motors. No matter which system you use, the process for making a basic shade applies, but it's a good idea to purchase the system first, to determine if any special processes or supplies are needed.

When mounting Roman shades on the wall outside of the window frame or opening, plan to extend 1 inch (2.5 cm) beyond each side of the window and several inches above if you can, to expose more window view when the shade is lifted. For inside-mounted Roman shades, allow ¼ inch (6 mm) clearance on each side.

(continued)

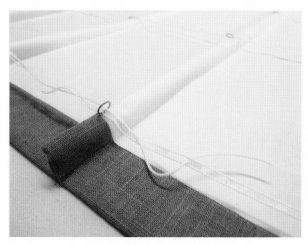

Shade cord is woven in and out of a cord shroud to prevent it from being pulled away from the back of the shade.

An assortment of shade rings in metal and plastic.

An example of two different lifting systems: track with interior spools and roller tube.

Roman shades look best when made slightly wider and several inches taller than the window.

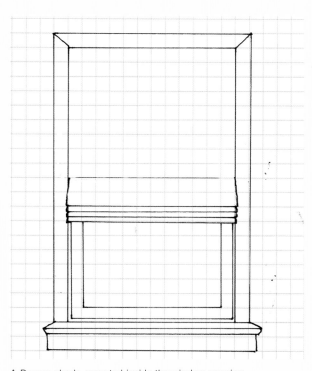

A Roman shade mounted inside the window opening.

WHAT YOU WILL NEED

- decorator fabric
- lining
- mounting board
- metal rod or wooden dowel
- heavy-duty stapler and staples
- sew-on Roman shade rings

- Safe-T-Shade RingLocks or cord shroud
- shade cord
- cord adjusting orbs
- lifting system
- tools and hardware for installation

YARDAGE REQUIREMENTS

To determine yardage, add allowances to the finished size as outlined below.

MAIN FABRIC

Measure your window and determine the finished width and length of your shade.

A. Finished length of shade _____ + 8 inches (15.2 cm) = _____ ÷ 36 inches (91.4 cm) = _____ yards (meters) of fabric

B. Finished width _____ + 8 inches (20.3 cm) = _____ ÷ fabric width = _____. If this number is greater than 1, double the amount from Step A.

If using more than one width of a print fabric, you may need to match the pattern motif, which could require additional fabric.

Finished length of shade = _____ + 8 inches (15.2 cm) = _____ ÷ pattern repeat = _____ (round up). This is how many of pattern repeats you will need for each cut.

Pattern repeat _____ × number of pattern repeats needed ÷ 36 inches (91.4 cm) = _____ yards (meters)

LINING FABRIC

A. Finished length of shade _____ + 2 inches (5 cm) = _____ ÷ 36 inches (91.4 cm) = _____ yards (meters)

B. Finished shade width = _____ ÷ fabric width = _____. If this number is greater than 1, double the amount from Step A.

When sewing multiple widths together, you may want to split widths in half lengthwise for a whole piece in the center, and sew half widths to each side. Study the pattern motif to determine what is best. For shades with a short length, you can railroad fabrics and linings. This will allow you to have a wide shade without any seams.

(continued)

MAKING A BASIC ROMAN SHADE

1 Cut the main fabric the finished width plus 8 inches (20.3 cm) wide and the finished length plus 6 inches (15.2 cm) long. For a large shade, seam together the fabric cuts and press seams open before cutting to size.

2 Place the main fabric face down, and fold over 4 inches (10.2 cm) along one side, iron in a crease, and then fold the cut edge under and press, creating a 2-inch (5 cm) doubled hem. Repeat for the other side and bottom hem, double-checking the measurement across the width of the shade.

3 At the bottom left and right corners, sew a mitered seam. This is optional; you can leave the bottom corners square. To create the mitered corner seam, unfold the pressed hems and measure 6 inches (15.2 cm) from the edge on one corner, making a mark at the center of the fold. **(A)** Draw a line from the inside corner to the outer corner, creating a right angle. **(B)** Fold the corner on the bias, pin, and stitch on the line. **(C)** Trim off excess fabric **(D)**, turn right sides out, and press. **(E)**

(continued)

Unfold the pressed hems at the corner. You will see the creases from pressing the hems. Measure 6 inches (15.2 cm) from the edge and mark in the center of the hem.

Draw a line, creating a right angle from the inside corner to the mark and out to the edge.

Fold the corner on the bias, lining up the cut edges and pinning together. Sew on the marked line.

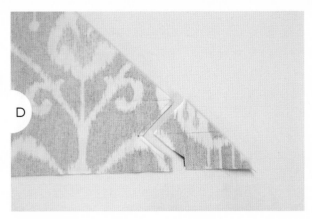

D

Cut off excess fabric.

E

Turn right sides out and press.

The finished corner is neat and has less bulk than the double-folded square corner.

4 Place the hemmed fabric facedown and top with the lining faceup, smoothing it out neatly. Trim off excess lining even with the side and bottom edges and tuck the edges under the hems. Secure the hems with pins. Hand sew the hems around all three sides or finish using your preferred method. (See Hemming, page 20.) Secure the top edge with pins. **(F)**

Cut the lining to the exact finished width and place it under the hems.

5 With the shade facedown, fold over 4 inches (10.2 cm) at the bottom and press. Draw a line 1 inch (2.5 cm) from the folded edge, pin, and straight stitch to create a rod pocket. **(G)**

A rod pocket is sewn above the bottom hem.

6 Mark for the rings on the back of the shade. Begin with the vertical spacing by measuring along the inside edge of the side hem, beginning at the rod pocket stitch line and measuring 7 inches (17.8 cm). Make a small mark on the lining next to the side hem. Measure from that mark up toward the top, spacing marks 8 inches (20.3 cm) apart, until you are within 12 inches (20.3 cm) or less of the finished length. Repeat for the opposite side. This will create 4-inch (10.2 cm) folds as the shade is lifted. You can adjust the vertical spacing. For example, if using 3-inch (7.6 cm) folds with the rings spaced 6 inches (15.2 cm) apart vertically, subtract 1 inch (2.5 cm) from the instructions above. **(H)**

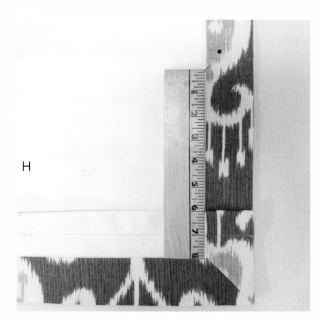

Mark 7 inches (17.8 cm) from the rod pocket stitch line and then continue marking every 8 inches (20.3 cm) to the top of the shade.

7 Next, mark for horizontal spacing of the
rings across the shade. Measure between
the outer marks at the side hems and divide by
a number that will result in 9 inches (22.9 cm)
or less. Mark across the top edge of the rod
pocket and continue from the bottom to the
top marks. (I)

8 Pin together the face fabric and lining at
each mark to hold the layers together. Sew a
shade ring at each mark using a thread to match
the face, sewing all the way through to the front
and removing the pins. Rings can be hand sewn
or machine sewn using a button-sewing attachment. The rings should be sewn so that they are
parallel with the top and bottom. Make sure the
bottom rings sewn to the rod pocket are secure,
as they will bear the weight of the shade. (J)

9 Cut a metal rod or wooden dowel 1 inch
(2.5 cm) less than the finished width and
insert inside the rod pocket. Sew or glue the ends
of the pocket closed. (K)

(continued)

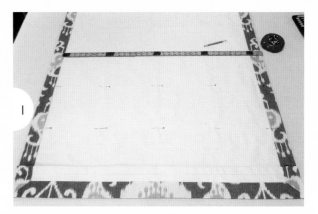

Create a template for ring spacing on a straight edge or ruler with
marked pieces of tape. Move the template from row to row. This
will save time!

Make sure the bottom rings sewn to the rod pocket are secure,
as they will bear the weight of the shade.

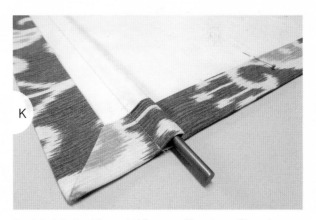

A painted steel rod is needed for some lift systems. The extra
weight creates tension needed for the system to engage.
Otherwise, an aluminum rod or wooden dowel will work just fine.

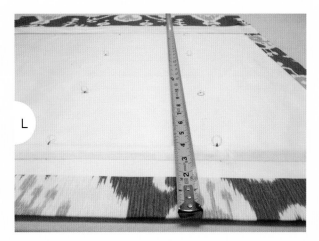

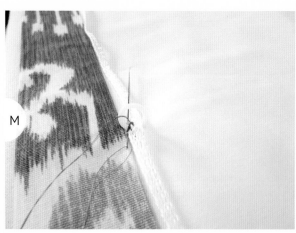

For the most accurate length, measure after the rings are sewn and the rod is inserted in the pocket.

Sew the cord shroud at each ring. Do not stitch over the cord within.

10 With the shade facedown, measure from the bottom to the top, folding over at the finished length and pressing to create a crease. Cut off excess fabric, allowing for 2 inches (5 cm) past the crease line for attaching to the board. (L)

This shade uses a cord shroud tube to meet safety standards. The tube is stitched in place at each ring. (M) You can sew rings and shroud all at the same time. Tie off the shroud to the top and bottom rings. The cord within the tube is fished out at the bottom and fastened with a cord-adjusting orb. (N) At the top ring, the cord is fished out of the shroud tube and threaded into the lifting system.

Note: Some cord shrouds are made without the cord and you will thread the cord into the shroud.

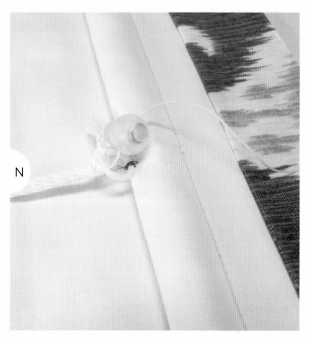

Fish the cord from the shroud and secure with an orb.

11 Cut the board to the finished width. Cover the ends of the board with the face fabric. Draw a line on top of the board 2 inches (5 cm) from the edge and staple the shade to the board at the line. Continue covering the board, hiding cut edges and staples. (See page 113.)

12 Attach the shade lifting system to the board and thread the cords into the system.

13 Install the shade to the wall using angle irons or the brackets supplied with the lifting system. (See Installing Window Treatments, pages 109–122.) Some fabrics require training to fall into neat folds. To do this, pull the shade to the highest position and steam. Smooth over the fabrics, creasing with your hands along the horizontal folds.

Cords run from the bottom to the top within the shroud, lifting the shade.

RELAXED ROMAN SHADE

A relaxed Roman shade is less structured and has a softer look than a flat shade. The objective is to add a small amount of fullness, providing enough ease for the bottom hem to swag slightly. This can be achieved in several ways: by cutting the shade with a flared bottom section, by adding small pleats to each end, by adding one pleat in the center, or by angling the rings wider at the bottom.

GETTING STARTED

In this tutorial you will learn how to make a relaxed shade by cutting the bottom wider, in a fishtail shape. This is one of the easiest shades to make! These shades are non-working and set in a fixed position. Boards with Velcro are used to make installation easy. Stationary shades like this are the perfect choice for children's rooms—there are no hazardous cords and they are easy to remove for cleaning.

If you would like the shade to be operable, this method is a good choice because the body of the shade is made straight and square; only the bottom section is shaped. The shade will stack up into neat folds above the relaxed hem.

This version of a Roman shade has soft folds at the bottom hem.

WHAT YOU WILL NEED

- decorator fabric
- lining
- mounting board
- wooden dowel
- ¾-inch (1.8 cm) sew-on Velcro (hook and loop)

- heavy-duty stapler and staples
- small cable ties
- sew-on Roman shade rings
- tools and hardware for installation

YARDAGE REQUIREMENTS

MAIN FABRIC

Measure your window and determine the finished width and length of your shade.

A. Finished length of shade ____ + 20½ inches (21.6 cm) = _____ ÷ 36 inches (91.4cm) = _____ yards (meters) of fabric

B. Finished width _____ + 4 inches (10.2 cm) = _____ ÷ fabric width = _____. If this number is greater than 1, double the amount from Step A.

If using more than one width of a print fabric, you may need to match the pattern motif, which could require additional fabric.

Finished length of shade = ____ + 20½ inches (21.6 cm) = _____ ÷ pattern repeat = _____ (round up). This is how many of pattern repeats you will need for each cut.

Pattern repeat ____ × number of pattern repeats needed ÷ 36 inches (91.4cm) = _____ yards (meters)

LINING FABRIC

A. Finished length of shade ____ + 20½ inches (21.6 cm) = _____ ÷ 36 inches (91.4cm) = _____ yards (meters)

B. Finished shade width = _____ + 4 inches (10.2 cm) ÷ fabric width = _____. If this number is greater than 1, double the amount from Step A.

When sewing multiple widths together, you may want to split widths in half lengthwise for a whole piece in the center, and sew half widths to each side. Study the pattern motif to determine what is best. For shades with a short length, you can railroad fabrics and linings. This will allow you to have a wide shade without any seams.

(continued)

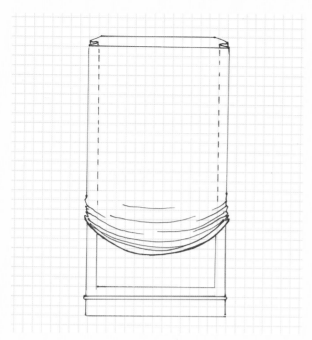

Small pleats are added at each side to create the fullness needed for the relaxed, swag bottom hem.

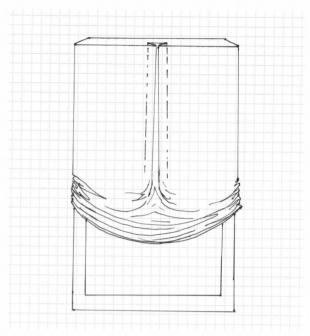

One pleat can be used in the center to create a relaxed shade. Use minimal fullness; too large of a pleat will make the shade droop and look baggy in the center.

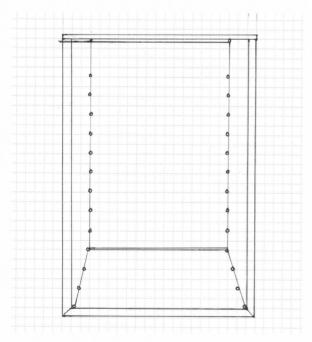

Back view of a Roman shade with rings angled wider at the bottom to create a relaxed style. The weight bar matches the width of the rings in the body of the shade.

MAKING A RELAXED
ROMAN SHADE

1 Measure the window to determine the finished width. For an inside-mounted shade, deduct ¼ inch (6 mm). Measure an approximate finished length; it can be adjusted later.

2 Fold the fabric lengthwise, right sides together. Starting at the bottom, measure and mark as shown in the diagram (a) half the finished width plus 2 inches (5 cm), (b) 18½ inches (47 cm), and (c) half the finished width plus 1 inch (2.5 cm), which will continue to the top. Cut and unfold. **(A)**

3 Place the lining faceup and top with the cut face fabric, facedown. Cut the lining to fit and pin to hold the edges together. Sew the side and bottom edges using a ½-inch (1.3 cm) seam allowance.

4 Turn right sides out and press the front and back, making sure the edges are flat and neat. **(B)**

(continued)

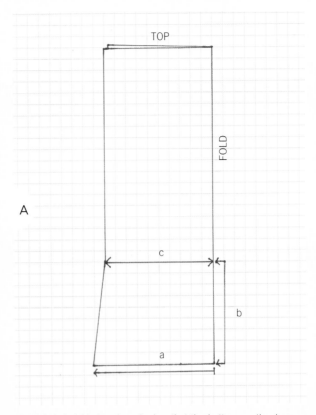

The fabric is folded and marked so that the bottom section is wider than the main body of the shade.

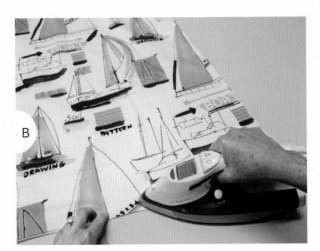

Press from the front, making sure the lining doesn't peek out from behind the edges.

5 Place the shade facedown and mark ring placement from the bottom, 1 inch (2.5 cm) from the edge and 6 inches (15.2 cm) apart. Continue to the height needed for a stationary shade, or to within 12 inches (30.5 cm) of the finished length for a working shade. Repeat for the opposite side.

6 Sew shade rings at each mark, catching the face fabric with the stitches. (C)

7 Measure from the bottom to the top and mark at the finished length plus ¾ inch (1.8 cm). Cut away any excess fabric. On the front top edge, pin Velcro loop strip and ma chine sew to the shade. (D) Fold over and hand sew the Velcro to the back. (E) You can also machine sew, but the stitches will show from the front.

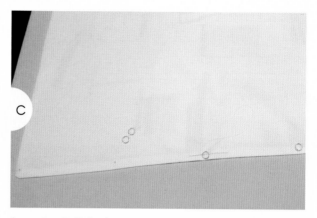

On a relaxed shade, rings are used only on the outer edges.

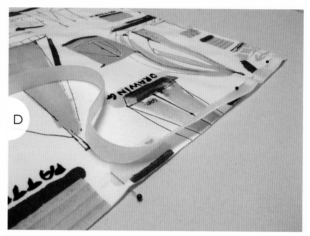

Velcro loop strip is pinned and then machine sewn to the front.

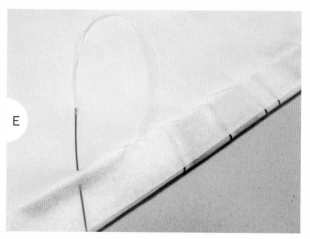

The Velcro is folded under to the reverse side and secured with hand sewing. Do not catch the face fabric with the stitches.

8 Cut a wooden dowel 2 inches (5 cm) less than the finished width and cover with a sleeve of lining and hand sew above the rings at the top of the angled bottom section. This will keep the shade from pulling in at the sides. (F)

9 Cinch together the four shade rings at the bottom section, plus additional rings up the side to achieve the desired length using a small cable tie. If making a working shade, cinch together only the bottom four rings to create stationary folds. (G)

10 Cut the board to the finished width. Cover with lining and staple Velcro hook strip to the front. Install the board at the window and attach the shade. (H) (See Installing Window Treatments, pages 109–122.) Smooth the folds at the bottom of the shade so that they hang evenly.

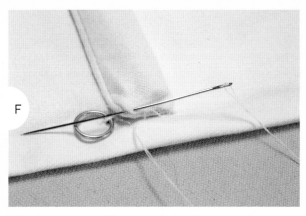

F

A fabric-covered dowel is sewn to the outside edges to keep the shade from pulling in on each side.

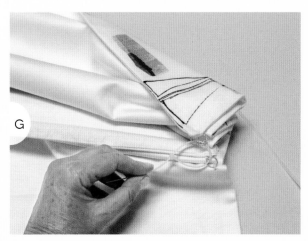

G

Small cable ties are used to cinch together the shade rings on each side.

H

Cut off excess cable tie. The shade is ready to install.

TOP TREATMENTS

Top treatments are purely decorative, adding color, pattern, and beautiful shapes to the tops of windows. Swags, cornice boards, and pleated and gathered valances all serve as top treatments. Pair with draperies or shades to create a stunning overall design.

Many techniques for curtains and shades are used when making top treatments, only they're scaled to fit above the window. Many top treatments are mounted to boards, but decorative hardware can be used as well. There are endless possibilities.

GATHERED VALANCE

Valances should be mounted above the window, raised up above and covering the top of the frame and a few inches of the window glass. Avoid a top-heavy appearance. Scale drawings or paper patterns can be used to determine good proportions.

Since top treatments and valences are viewed from below, be conscious of the lining and edge finishes. It looks more attractive to have a matching or contrast color for the lining and trims such as welt cords, ruffles, or fringe along the bottom.

Rod pocket valances are very popular and can be installed on decorative hardware or plain white utility rods. For this valance, a white pole rod with finials was used, and you will see a clever solution for adding a return to the rod pocket, so that the valance looks neat and finished at the sides.

GETTING STARTED

Select light- to medium-weight fabrics. Complementary fabric should be used for the lining because it will show at the short points. A small covered welt cord in the seam makes turning the edges easier and gives a polished look. Fringe or banding can also be used to embellish the bottom edge.

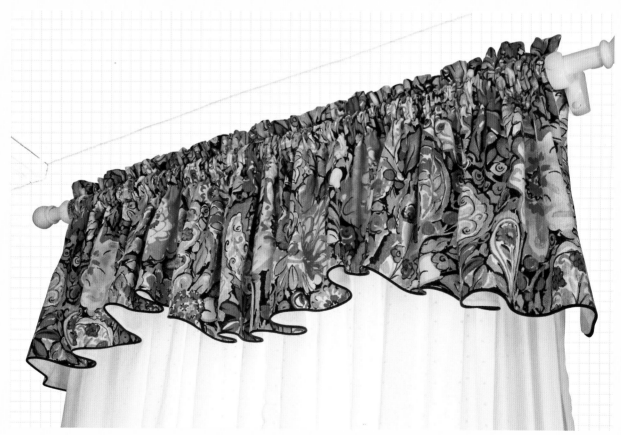

This pretty floral valance is gathered on a pole rod.

WHAT YOU WILL NEED

+ decorator fabric
+ lining

+ small-diameter welt cord
+ tools and hardware for installation

YARDAGE REQUIREMENTS

MAIN FABRIC AND LINING

Measure your window and determine the finished width, long point, and short point. For solid or allover patterns, the fabric can be cut on the straight, or railroaded. Plan for two and half times fullness. Lining fabric can be railroaded even if the face fabric is not.

For the rod pocket, measure around the pole or rod with a flexible tape measure. Do not make the rod pocket too tight; it should slide on and off the rod easily. For the ruffle above the rod pocket, allow 1 to 3 inches (2.5 to 7.6 cm). Add together the rod pocket and top ruffle and multiply times two. Use this for the calculations at right (rod pocket and top ruffle).

Finished width ___ + returns ___ × 2.5 fullness = ___ ÷ fabric width = ___ number of cuts needed

Finished length (longest point) ___ + rod pocket and top ruffle ___ + ½ inch (1.3 cm) seam allowance = cut length

Number of cuts × cut length = ___ ÷ 36 inches (91.4 cm) = ___ yards (meters)

If using a fabric with a pattern repeat, take this into consideration for the cut length.

Cut length = ___ ÷ pattern repeat = ___ (round up) = number of pattern repeats for each cut

Pattern repeat ___ × number of pattern repeats for each cut = _____ cut length adjusted for pattern matching

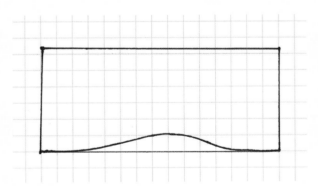

Draw a pattern for half the valance shape.

(continued)

MAKING A GATHERED VALANCE

1 Cut a piece of muslin or pattern paper the finished cut length of the valance × 1.25 the width. This will be half of the finished valance. Mark the short point and long points and draw a curved line between the marks.

2 Cut the fabrics and seam together. Press the seams open.

3 Fold over a doubled hem or heading across the top of the seamed face fabric for the rod pocket and ruffle heading. For example, if your rod pocket is 2 inches (5 cm) and the ruffle is 1 inch (2.5 cm), you will make a 3-inch (7.6 cm) heading, requiring 6 inches (15.2 cm) of fabric.

4 Press the doubled heading and then fold the valance in half, face together, neat and square.

5 Use the pattern to draw the curved shape across the bottom, adding a ½-inch (1.3 cm) seam allowance, and cut the curved shape. (A)

6 Cover enough small-diameter welt cord to go across the bottom edge. Sew to the bottom edge, following the curved shape.

7 Place the face fabric with welt cord attached facedown on the lining that is faceup. Smooth, straighten, and press. Pin together the bottom edge for sewing. (B)

A

Cut the curved shape across the bottom of the valance fabric.

B

Pin the front piece with welt cord attached to the lining.

8 Sew across the bottom edge, stitching close to the welt cord. Sew each end using a ½-inch (1.3 cm) seam allowance. Leave the top open.

9 Cut away excess fabric below the welt cord. Cut close to the cord, leaving a ¼-inch (6 mm) seam allowance. (C)

10 Turn the valance right sides out. Press from the front and back. (D)

11 With the valance facedown, fold over the top rod pocket and ruffle heading. Press and pin for sewing. Draw a line to follow the ruffle along the back of the heading. Sew two rows of stitching: the bottom edge of the doubled heading and along the line drawn for the top ruffle. (E)

12 Use a compensating foot or walking foot on the machine to keep the layers of fabric from bunching up as you sew. If you don't have specialty feet for your machine, make small tucks in the fabric as you sew. The tucks will be on the back and they will not show when the valance is gathered.

(continued)

Cut off excess fabric below the welt cord.

Press the edges and the entire valance front and back.

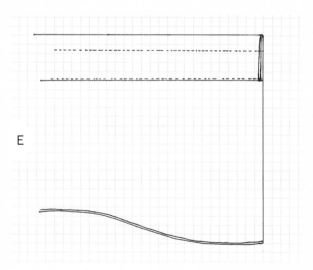

Sew two horizontal rows of stitching, one at the bottom edge of the pocket and one above to create the bottom of the ruffle.

13 For valances on pole rods with finials and brackets, a return is needed. To do this, measure and mark the size of the return on the rod pocket, on the front of the valance. **(F)**

14 Carefully cut a slit in the face fabric and one layer of lining below. Do not cut all the way through. **(G)**

15 Tuck under the cut edges and use fabric glue to finish like a buttonhole. Just use a little glue to finish the edges. You don't want to glue together the rod pocket! **(H)**

Mark the distance for the return from the rod to the wall.

Cut a slit through the face fabric and one layer of lining and tuck under the edges.

Add a little fabric glue to hold the cut folded edges together like a buttonhole.

16 Slide the rod from the front into one of the holes cut in the rod pocket and out the other, gathering the valance on the rod. (I)

17 Install on the window with brackets. Dress the valance so it is evenly gathered. (See Installing Window Treatments, pages 109–122.)

Slide the rod into the pocket.

Black welt cord outlines the bottom shape.

UPHOLSTERED SOFT CORNICE WITH INSET BANDING

Cornice boards are typically constructed of wood, and while they are a beautiful style and fun to make, they can be quite heavy and difficult to install. A soft cornice, which uses a stiff interfacing instead of plywood, gives the same look with less weight, doesn't require as many woodworking tools, and can be attached to the mount board with staples or Velcro, allowing for more flexibility for difficult sizes and shapes of windows. This is mostly a no-sew project.

GETTING STARTED

Select fabrics that can that can be ironed with high heat and steam. Avoid thin, stretchy, or shiny fabrics, as they will not perform well with the adhesives and glue.

This is a lightweight version of a cornice, but it looks like it's made of wood.

WHAT YOU WILL NEED

- decorator fabric
- blackout lining
- pattern paper
- stiff polyester interfacing like Peltex or Skirtex
- polyester fusible fleece
- fusible web like Wonder-Under
- fabric glue

- welt cord
- gimp braid trim
- wooden board
- Sealah double-sided adhesive flat shaper wire
- heavy-duty stapler and staples
- pushpins
- tools and hardware for installation

YARDAGE REQUIREMENTS

If using a print fabric, additional fabric may be needed to match the pattern motif.

Finished width + 4 inches (10.2 cm) ÷ fabric width = number of widths

Finished length + top + 4 inches (10.2 cm) = cut length

Number of widths × cut length ÷ 36 inches (91.4 cm) = number of yards (meters) needed

Additional yardage is needed for bias strips for welt cord.

For this project, the reverse sides of the returns are covered in lining. If your cornice has an angled design, you may want to cover the inside of the return areas with face fabric because it may show when viewed from below. Allow extra to the width when estimating the yardage.

Shaped, inset banding is made by wrapping fabric around a piece of iron-on interfacing cut to the finished shape. A heavy interfacing or buckram can be used for cornice boards.

(continued)

Cut fusible interfacing to the finished shape and apply to the back of the banding fabric. Cut around the interfacing, leaving a ½-inch (1.3 cm) seam allowance on the top and bottom edges.

Clip the edges, fold over, and glue to the back.

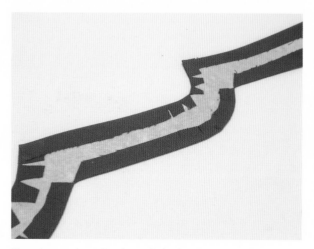

The edges are turned under and glued to the back.

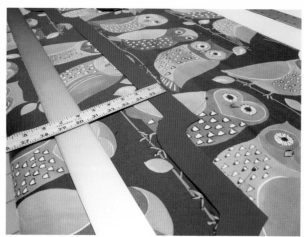

Glue or sew the banding to the main fabric.

1 Draw the finished banding shape on fusible interfacing and cut out. Iron the shaped piece to the back of the banding fabric. For large projects, the fabric may need to be seamed together. Overlap the interfacing slightly if it is cut in pieces. (A)

2 Clip around curves and corners, turning and pressing the edges over the interfacing. Glue the cut edges to the back. (B)

MAKING AN UPHOLSTERED SOFT CORNICE WITH INSET BANDING

1 Cornice board designs can be any shape, from scallops to stair-stepped right angles. Look in books, magazines, and online photo-sharing sites for inspiration. Often the fabric will inspire a design. Draw a scale drawing of the pattern on graph paper is a great first step to experiment with shapes and styles.

Using your measurements for the width and long and short points, draw at least half of the pattern of the finished cornice (face only, not the sides) on brown craft paper, or pattern paper. Make the finished size ½ inch (1.3 cm) wider to allow for take-up of the thick layers. At the top and sides, add the size of the board to the pattern, making a cutout at the left and right top corners. (A)

2 Glue inset banding to the face fabric using the pattern and rulers to make sure it is lined up properly. Banding or other trims can also be added later, after the cornice is constructed but before board mounting. (B)

3 Use the pattern to draw and cut one each of Peltex, fusible fleece, and adhesive web.

4 With the fabric facedown, top with the fleece, adhesive side down. Iron the fleece to the fabric, centering pattern motifs and keeping the fabric neat and flat. Use a "press cloth" (a scrap of cotton lining or muslin) so the fleece will not stick to the iron. After the fleece is attached, turn the fabric over and press from the front. Try to use only one piece of fleece. If your project is larger than the fleece, butt pieces together at the board line, or returns, but not in the center front of the cornice. (C)

(continued)

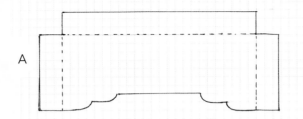

Draw the pattern, adding for the returns and top.

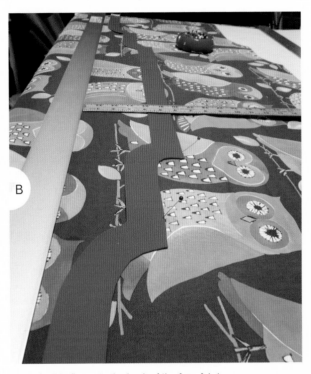

Apply fusible fleece to the back of the face fabric.

Shaped banding is glued to the fabric.

5 Apply the fusible web to the back of the Peltex by ironing with the paper-backing side up. After it is completely ironed and cooled, peel away the paper backing. You can butt together pieces of the fusible web if one whole piece is not large enough. (D)

6 Place the Peltex with the adhesive backing to the fleece, which is attached to the back of the face fabric. Line up the pieces so the shapes match. (E) Iron the pieces together using a press cloth. (F)

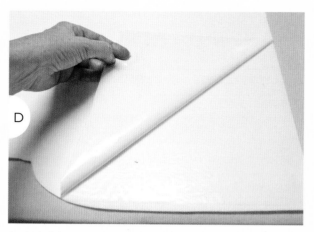

Apply fusible web to the back of the Peltex and peel away the paper backing.

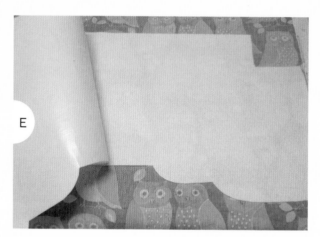

Place the Peltex adhesive side down over the fleece.

Iron the Peltex to the fleece, joining them together.

7 Trim away excess fabric along the bottom edge to 1½ to 2 inches (3.8 to 5 cm). Glue the cut edges to the back of the Peltex using fabric glue. Make relief cuts at the corners, and clip around curves as needed. Pin in place and let dry. (G)

8 Make bias-covered welt cord. Cut additional strips of fabric on the bias 2½ inches (6.4 cm) wide, join the pieces together, and sew to the welt cord, getting close so all the stitching is hidden. (H) This will be used as a facing along the reverse of the cornice. (I)

(continued)

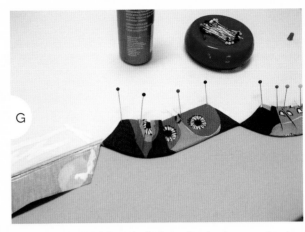

Trim away excess fabric at the bottom edge, leaving enough extra fabric to turn under and glue to the back.

Sew a bias strip to the welt cord, getting close the cord to hide the stitching.

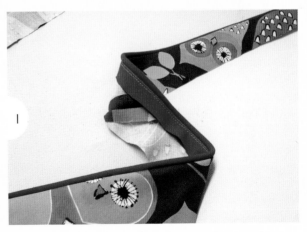

The facing strip hides the stitches.

9 Glue the welt cord along the bottom edge, following the design. Make sure no stitching shows. Pin and let dry. (J)

10 Turn the piece over and glue the facing to the back, making relief cuts and clipping as needed. (K) The shape of this cornice has sharp corners, which require a deep relief cut. Small patches of matching fabric are used to cover the corners. (L)

Glue the welt cord to the bottom edge.

Glue the facing to the back.

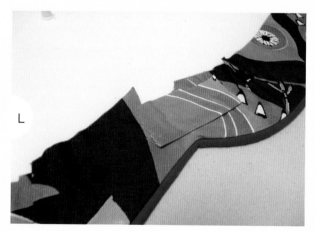

A small patch of matching fabric covers the corner relief cut.

11 Add pieces of Sealah double-sided adhesive flat shaper wire to the bottom edges at each return, inset about 2 inches (5 cm) from the bottom. This will let you shape the return at a right angle. If you don't have this product, you can attach an L-bracket with double-sided tape or pieces of florist wire. The goal is to add something that will create a right angle for the return. (M)

12 Cover the back with blackout lining. Trim the lining 1 inch (2.5 cm) shorter on the back bottom edge. (N) At each side, turn over the face fabric and glue to the Peltex, and then turn under the lining and glue. (O)

(continued)

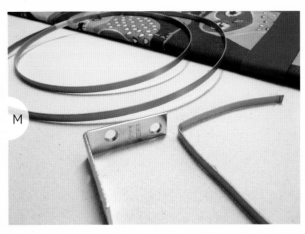

Use Sealah shaper or L-brackets to create a right angle at each side return.

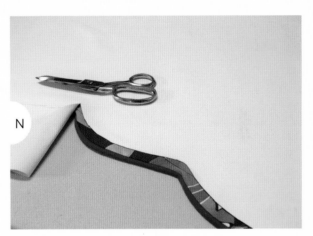

Cut the blackout lining 1 inch (2.5 cm) less than the bottom edge.

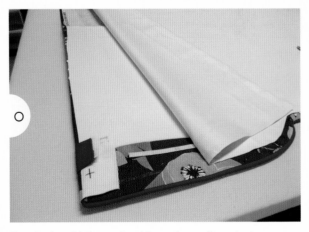

Turn the face fabric over the sides and cover the cut edges with lining.

13 Glue gimp braid over the cut edge of the lining on the back, at the bottom of the cornice. (P)

14 At each end, fold over the size needed for the return, and press with heat and steam. This will help the cornice bend into shape. Repeat for the top.

15 Cover the mounting board with lining. Staple the soft cornice to the board (Q), turning under the cut edges and trimming away excess fabric. (R) If areas are bulky, trim away Peltex or fleece to fit the board.

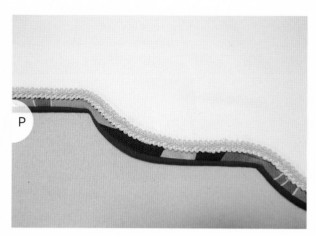

Glue gimp braid over the cut edge of the lining.

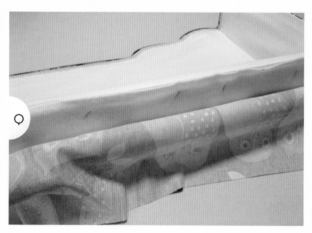

Staple the Peltex and fleece at the top of the board.

Cut away excess fabric at the corners.

16 Staple across the back edge of the board and glue the top edges. (S)

17 Install to the wall using L-brackets. (See Installing Window Treatments, pages 109–122.)

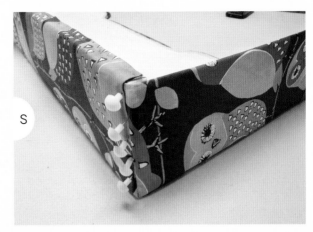

S

Turn under the cut edges, glue, and hold in place with pushpins until the glue dries.

Contrast welt cord and banding are eye-catching details.

INSTALLATION

You have picked out the perfect fabrics, designed and constructed a beautiful window treatment, and now it's time to get it up on the window! Often this is a very simple task using basic tools, but some projects, such as two-story windows, require extra time, effort, and specialty equipment.

In this section you will learn the basics of board mounting, traverse hardware, and hanging and dressing. You will learn not only how to put curtains up on the window but also tricks for dressing and training fabrics for a fabulous finish!

Installation is the final step, but it's not something that just happens at the end of the project. Start thinking about and planning the installation from the very beginning when you measure and select fabrics and hardware, and throughout the process of sewing and finishing. Being prepared and ready for the installation is the key to a successful and beautiful finished window treatment.

types of hardware

There are many styles and types of hardware, from simple utility rods to elaborate decorative poles. Choosing the best hardware for your project is based on the use and purpose of the window treatment. If you want to open and close curtains, purchase traversing hardware. For stationary curtains, a simple extension rod can be used.

With decorative hardware, the style and finish are important parts of the overall design. Examples include painted or stained wood, metal, iron, and even glass and acrylic in traditional and contemporary designs.

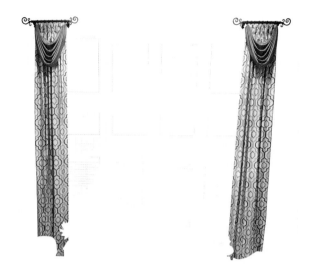

This photo with the swag and drapery is an illustration of a two-story window.

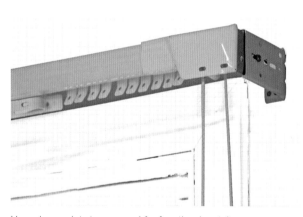

Use a heavy-duty traverse rod for functional curtains.

The right hardware makes a statement! This rod made with industrial pipe is perfect for a modern loft. The same curtain would look much different with a traditional wooden pole rod.

mounting boards

Many window treatments are board mounted. This is one of the most common ways to install top treatments and valances, but curtains and shades can also be mounted to boards.

Boards should be covered or painted so they look neat and clean, and secured to the wall or window trim with L-brackets. Use a bracket that is larger than half the board projection. For example, use at least a 2-inch (5 cm) bracket to install a 3½-inch (8.9 cm) board.

The brackets are installed to the wall and the board is set on top, and then fastened with screws. Use an appropriate number of brackets for the size and weight of the window treatment. There should be a bracket placed every 36 to 48 inches (91.4 to 122 cm).

The window treatment can be stapled to the board or attached with hook-and-loop tape so it can be removed. When stapling the window treatment directly to the board, make sure all the staples and cut edges are covered. This is especially important if the top of the board can be viewed from a balcony or stairway. The following instructions will show you several different ways to cover mount boards.

Use L-brackets to install mount boards.

COVERING A BASIC MOUNT BOARD

1 Cut a piece of fabric large enough to wrap around the board and overlap 1 inch (2.5 cm) the length of the board plus 4 inches (10.2 cm). Wrap the fabric over each end and staple. (A)

2 Wrap the fabric over the top, folding corners in neatly, and staple. (B)

3 Overlap the fabric and staple to finish. (C)

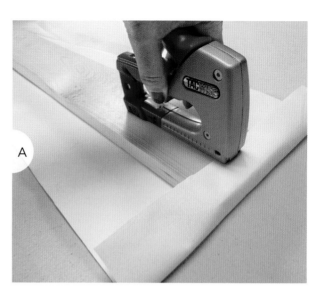

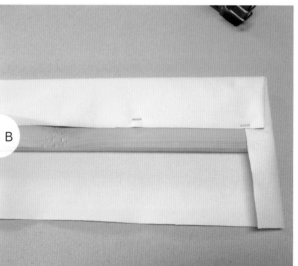

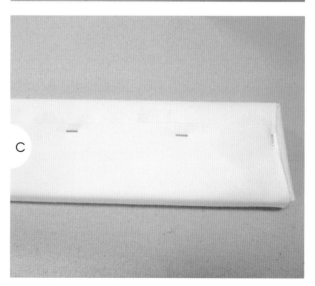

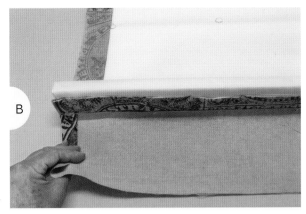

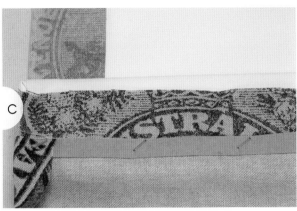

Attaching to a Mount Board: Option 1

1 Cover the board with matching fabric and staple the window treatment to the top. (A)

2 Cut a piece of matching fabric large enough to wrap around and 2 inches (5 cm) longer than the board. Place the fabric facedown along the front edge and staple to the board using cardboard tack strip. Fold over each end and staple. (B)

3 Flip the fabric over the tack strip. (C) The tack strip creates a crisp and even edge. (D)

4 Fold under the cut edges and staple to the back edge of the board. The staples will be on the edge that is against the wall.

Attaching to a Mount Board: Option 2

1 Cover each end of the board with fabric. (A)

2 Staple the window treatment on top of the board. This window treatment wraps around the ends. (B)

3 Staple covered welt cord to the top front edge. This is optional; you can continue without welt cord. (C)

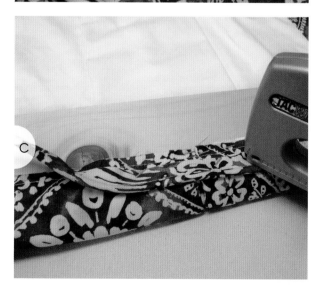

4 Cut a piece of matching fabric large enough to cover the top and wrap entirely around the board plus extra on each end to turn under. Staple facedown with cardboard tack strip. (D)

5 Fold the fabric under at each end and glue under the fold, or use a double-sided adhesive tape to finish the ends. (E)

6 Continue wrapping the fabric around the board to the opposite edge, hidden under the back of the window treatment. Tuck under the cut edges and staple. (F)

D

E

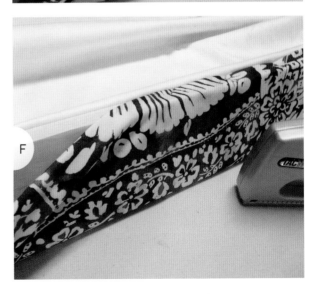

F

Another option for mounting to boards is to sew a band to the top. You can then staple the band to a covered board, or attach with hook-and-loop tape. In the example at right, the banding is sewn to a pleated valance, but it can also be used for shades, swags, jabots, and board-mounted curtains. Be sure to add for the seam allowance when marking and cutting the finished length of the window treatment.

SEWING A TOP BAND FOR BOARD MOUNTING

1 Cut a strip of matching fabric 3½ inches (8.9 cm) by the finished size needed plus 2 inches (5 cm). Use a serger or an overcast stitch to finish one long edge.

2 Place the strip facedown and pin the cut edge (not the serged edge) to the top, turning under 1 inch (2.5 cm) on each end to the back. Sew to the top using a ½-inch (1.3 cm) seam allowance. (A)

3 Fold the banding up and press from the front. (B)

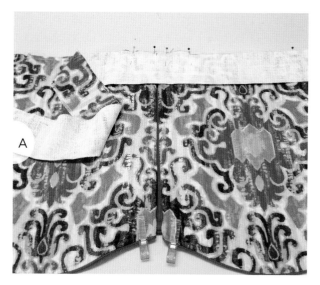

A

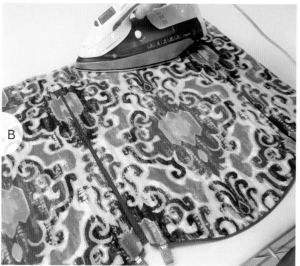

B

4 Turn the window treatment facedown. Add fabric glue to the top along the seam allowance. (C)

5 Fold the band over the glue and press. The glue will hold the banding in place until it is sewn. This is easier than pinning! (D)

(continued)

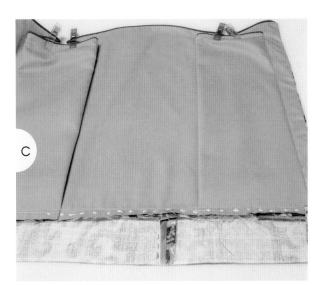

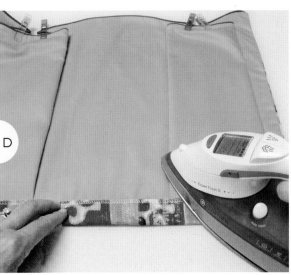

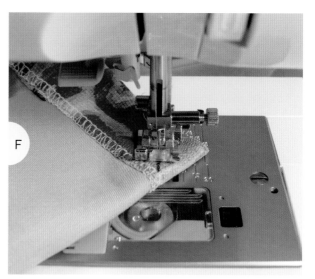

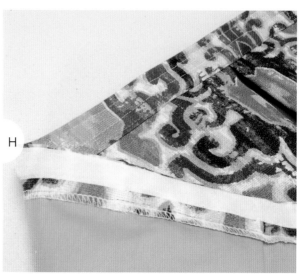

6 Sew across the banding from the top. (E)

7 At each end, fold over the return allowance and stitch at a 45-degree angle across the band to create a square corner. (F) (G)

8 Sew loop strip to the underside of the band. Hook strip is stapled to the board. (H)

When installing stationary curtains under board-mounted valances, screw eyes can be added under the board for drapery pins.

installation tools and tips

The key to a successful installation is preparation and patience. Every window is unique and every window treatment is different. You might be installing hardware into walls with wood studs and sheetrock or plaster and lathe, wood, metal, or concrete.

Some styles, such as cornice boards, can be tricky to install because of the limited space between the front of the cornice and the wall. An extension is needed on the drill to reach up into the tight space to screw the brackets to the mount board. Two-story windows or windows over stairways will need extension ladders and, in some cases, mechanical lifts to complete the installation.

Be aware of what might be inside the wall, such as water pipes and electrical wires, and glass when installing on doors.

Installing window treatments is often a job that is best left to a professional who has the knowledge and experience to complete the job safely and properly. The end goal is to have window treatments that will function easily and hang beautifully for years and years.

But don't be intimidated! Many window treatments are easy to install, and you will feel quite accomplished when you step back and admire your new window dressings.

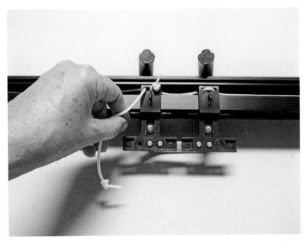

Pull out the cords to the length needed, setting the master carriers into the correct position.

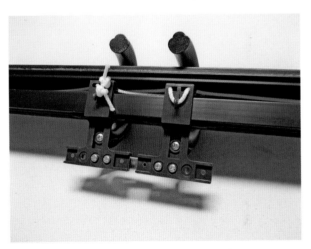

Set the position by looping the cord under the hook.

Before you begin the installation, put together a kit with all the tools and hardware that you will need. Typical items you will need include a ladder, screws, drill and drill bits, tape measure, level, awl, and pencil. Different surfaces require different types of screws, anchors, and fasteners. It's best to use Phillips or hex-head screws with the appropriate driver for your drill or screwdriver.

Familiarize yourself with the manufacturer's instructions and preassemble the hardware if necessary.

Measure and mark for the bracket placement based on the size of the window treatment. Use an awl to poke gently into the wall to see whether it is solid or hollow. You can also drill a small hole first, before setting screws—this is an important step on hollow walls or doors. Be sure to use a drill bit that is smaller than the screw size.

Continue installing the hardware, checking to make sure it is level. Sometimes the hardware is level but the ceiling or floor is not! Make subtle adjustments to make the window treatment appear level to the eye.

Adjust cord-draw traverse rods at the back of the master carriers, pulling out the cord to the length needed, setting the master carriers to the center, and then cutting off and knotting the cord. Once the cord is the correct length, set the cord to a fixed position by looping it over the small hook on the opposite carrier.

On window coverings with cords, be sure to follow the manufacturer's instructions for installing safety devices, and use them properly. Read any attached warning labels. It is best practice to use only cord-free window coverings in homes where children live or visit. Safety first, decorating second!

HELPFUL TIPS

+ Add double-sided tape to the back of brackets to temporarily hold the bracket to the wall. This will free up your hands for holding screws and drilling.

+ Use silicone spray to lubricate traverse rods, and wipe it along the top of decorative poles so rings move back and forth easier.

+ A drill with a magnetic driver will help prevent screws from slipping away and dropping to the floor.

+ Make a cardboard template for bracket placement when there are multiple windows of the same size and using the same hardware.

+ Wear a tool apron.

+ Secure returns on curtains and valances by installing a tenterhook or screw eye in the wall for the pin hook (as shown in photos).

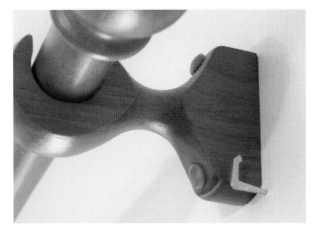

Use a tenterhook to hold the return.

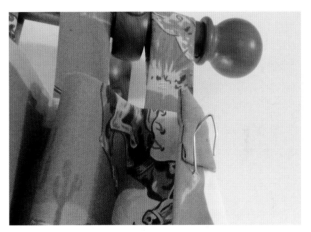

Insert a pin hook into the fabric at the return and hook over the tenterhook.

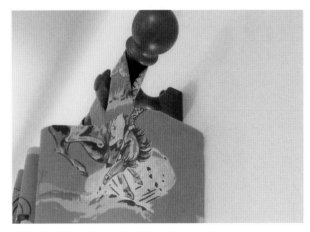

Curtains look best when the fabric returns to the wall.

hanging and dressing window treatments

After the window treatment is installed, it will need to be dressed to neaten the fold and drape of the fabric. To dress curtains, smooth the fabric with your hands and use a steamer to remove wrinkles. An oven mitt can be worn and the fabric lightly pressed against the mitt for more stubborn wrinkles.

On traverse rods with curtains where the hardware is behind the top heading, crease the spaces between the pleats forward. On decorative rods where the top heading is below the rings, the spaces between pleats can be creased to the back or brought forward.

Open the curtains to the side and work down each pleat, using your hands to straighten. After the curtains are arranged neatly, tie wide strips of muslin around the curtain from the top to the bottom, holding the curtain together. Tie the bands snug but not too tight or they will crease the fabric. Let the curtains stay bound overnight or for a few days. This will train the folds.

For Roman shades, pull up to the highest position and smooth horizontally with your hands, creating even folds. Steam and let the shade stay in this position overnight. This will help the fabric refold neatly.

Manipulate the fabric on valances and top treatments by smoothing by hand and arranging pleats and folds to the desired look. A tag or tacking gun can be used to control flare by tacking inside pleats and folds.

glossary

Bead weight (aka sausage weight)—tiny weights that are encased inside a woven strip and added to the bottom curtains for an even weight across the entire hem. Bead weight can also be covered and used in place of welt cord in seams.

Blackout—a lining material that has been treated to block all light. Look for a three-pass blackout material for complete light blocking.

Board mount—installing a window treatment to a top board that is then secured to the wall.

Buckram—traditionally a woven cotton cloth stiffened with starch (aka crinoline), but modern versions can be made from polyester or heavy paper. Used to add structure in curtain and valance headings for crisp pleats. Buckram is available in different widths and sew-on or iron-on. The most common width is 4 inches (10.2 cm).

Bump cloth—a very heavy blanket-like interlining commonly used in silk for a luxurious finish.

Curtain or drapery panel—a panel is one piece of a curtain or drapery hung at the window. Panels can be single or multiple widths of fabric sewn together.

Decorative hardware—wooden or metal pole rods used for installing curtains and valances.

Dim out—also called thermal lining, this material has a suede-like surface that helps to diffuse light.

Finial—a decorative detail added to the end of pole rods.

French blackout—a method for creating blackout using face fabric layered with interlining, black lining, and an outer lining.

Fullness—the amount of extra fabric width needed to create pleats or gathers in a window treatment in relation to the size of the window or rod. A common fullness ratio used in window treatments is to multiple two and a half times the rod width.

Hand—the way a fabric feels when touched and draped.

Heading—the hem at the top of a drapery or valance that is shirred or pleated. A heading often has buckram, shirring tape, grommets, or other details to create a specific style.

Headrail—any system used to operate a blind or shade.

Interlining—usually flannel but can be any fabric that is sandwiched between the face fabric and lining.

Lining—a cotton, polyester and cotton blend, or polyester fabric used to cover the reverse side of a window treatment. Look for a lining material that is specifically finished for window treatments; they will perform better than other fabrics. Two common brands in the United States are Hanes Fabrics and Rockland Industries. Most common colors of lining are white, ivory, and khaki.

Medallions—decorative posts or knobs used at the top of draped window treatments or for tiebacks.

Railroading fabric—placing fabric so that it runs down the bolt instead of side to side. This is common in upholstery or when making valances and top treatments to eliminate seams. Some fabrics are printed with this orientation specifically for upholstery.

Repeat—how often the pattern motif on a fabric is duplicated. There are horizontal and vertical pattern repeats.

Return—the area on window treatments that wraps around the hardware or board flush to the wall to cover the projection.

Selvage—the finished edges along the length of the fabric.

Tabling—a term used in the workroom to describe laying out fabrics, measuring, and finishing pieces of a window treatment on the worktable.

Valance—a decorative window treatment that dresses the top of the window. A valance can be plain, pleated, shirred, or a swag style.

Weight tape—square weights sewn into a wide tape, most commonly used in hems of stage curtains and other heavy, large projects.

Weights—metal pieces that are square, round, or triangular in shape and added to hems and seams to help window treatments hang properly. Traditionally, weights are made of lead but newer versions are made of non-lead metal compounds and are safer for the environment.

resources

FABRICS, SEWING AND WORKROOM SUPPLIES
DraperySupplies.com
HanesFabrics.com
HomeSew.com
HomeSewingDepot.com
Joann.com
MaryJos.com
NancysNotions.com
RowleyCompany.com
Textol.com
Wawak.com

ADHESIVE TAPES
Dofix.com
Millenniumtape.com
DonnaSkufis.com

PROFESSIONAL WINDOW TREATMENT PATTERNS
Mfay.com
PateMeadows.com
PatternsPlus.com

HARDWARE
HelserBrothers.com
SafeTShade.com
UnitedSupplyCo.com

EDUCATION
Craftsy.com
HomeDecGal.com
TheWorkroomChannel.com

about the author

Susan Woodcock owns Home Dec Gal, a how-to sewing resource and custom workroom in western North Carolina, and is a Bluprint (formerly Craftsy) instructor and international speaker. Susan's comprehensive how-to book, *Singer® Sewing Custom Curtains, Shades and Top Treatments* was published in 2016.

Together with her husband, Rodger Walker, Susan co-produces the Custom Workroom Conference, an annual educational event and trade show. In 2017, Susan and Rodger founded Custom Workroom Technical Center or "Workroom Tech," a hands-on training facility dedicated to the workroom industry.

She credits her mother with teaching her to sew and inspiring her career of creativity.

www.homedecgal.com
www.customworkroomconference.com
www.workroomtech.com

index

the first time series

THE ABSOLUTE BEGINNER'S GUIDES

There's a first time for everything. Enjoy the journey
and achieve success with the First Time series!

**LEARN BY
DOING**

• • •

STEP-BY-STEP
BASICS
+
PROJECTS

First Time Knitting

978-1-58923-805-3

First Time Crochet

978-1-58923-825-1

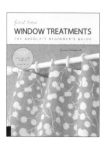

First Time Quilting

978-1-58923-824-4

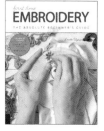

First Time Embroidery

978-1-63159-797-8

First Time Sewing

978-1-58923-804-6

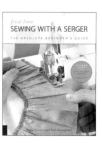

First Time Sewing with a Serger

978-1-63159-714-5

First Time Window Treatments

978-1-63159-785-5

First Time Garment Fitting

978-1-58923-962-3

First Time Cake Decorating

978-1-58923-961-6

First Time Jewelry Making

978-1-63159-698-8

First Time Felting

978-1-63159-803-6

128 pages | Paperback | Creative Publishing international QUARRY